Praise for *Oranges for Eve!*

"I just love every word, every page, everything about *Oranges for Eve*. It is inspiring, encouraging, and motivational. Women of all ages will just love it!"

> **Florine Mark**, president and chairman of the board,
> The WW Group, Inc. (Weight Watchers)

"Rabbi Tamara Kolton's *Oranges for Eve* is a stunning guidebook for women who are seeking to be spiritual activists in their lives. As she explains, "When we lost God in the feminine, we lost the ability to live the sacred circle that is life." Tamara offers a number of metaphors about feminine power and spirituality that have shaped our psyches for millennia. She also offers practical applications for emerging out of patriarchy and creating a world that fully honors the feminine. She skillfully outlines the ways in which self-hatred, body-shaming, and other ways of making ourselves small as women serve to alienate us from the sacred cycles of birth, death, and rebirth. Additionally, Tamara's interactive exercises help women to heal patterns of disempowerment, all while learning to step into new stories that uplift them and magnify their light. In the vein of Clarissa Pinkola Estés' *Women Who Run with the Wolves*, this is one of the most definitive books about feminine spirituality that I've read in years. *Oranges for Eve* is nothing short of a love song to feminine wholeness and the rich tapestry of women's personal and collective history, as well as where we get to go from here."

> **Kelly McNelis,** founder of Women For One,
> author of *Your Messy Brilliance*

"This is a personal narrative that at the same time carries a universal message. The book tells us how to navigate our world of growing, belonging, leaving, and growing again. It is told in strong, clear language. A must-read for any woman wanting to think about who she is and how she wishes to be in control of her own movement through life."

Glenda D. Price Ph.D.
President Emeritus, Marygrove College

"With this beautifully-written memoir and spiritual guide, Rabbi Tamara extends her hand and invites the reader to join her on a heroine's journey into the Sacred Divine. It wasn't until I read *Oranges for Eve* that I realized how much my spirit has been longing for a deeper connection to feminine truth, energy and personal strength. Rabbi Tamara is a fresh, young voice, but her wisdom is as old as Eve."

Anne Doyle, author of *POWERING UP: How America's Women Achievers Become Leaders*
global speaker, journalist, podcast host
president, International Women's Forum – Michigan
Michigan Journalism Hall of Fame

"An instant classic, this book should be required reading for all women intent on understanding their spiritual heritage. It's powerful. It's passionate. It's engaging. You'll find yourself opening your heart with cherished moments of profound understanding of what it truly means to be a woman. Highly recommended!"

Denise Linn, founder of The Red Lotus Women's Mystery School and author of *Secrets and Mysteries: The Glory and Pleasure of Being a Woman*

"*Oranges for Eve* tells an authentic and moving story; one that will touch your heart and open your soul. Tamara invites you to walk your path with confidence and pride. This book, like a delicious orange, not only quenches deep thirst, but is exquisite to behold."

Diane S. Blau, PhD, LP
President Emeritus
Michigan School of Psychology

"As a black woman, I was initially unsure of how I would relate to the experiences of a Jewish woman. However, Rabbi Tamara Kolton successfully removes the patriarchal veil that has impacted every segment of our lives. Tamara writes, 'What could be seen as more dangerous than a woman connected to the truth of who she really is?!' BOOM! From voting to reproductive rights, this book serves as a rally cry for modern women of all cultures."

Robin Kinnie, president of Motor City Woman Studios
and Audio Engineers of Detroit

"Rabbi Tamara Kolton Ph.D. has the rare gift of making everyone 'SPARKLE!' She is the teacher who guides women to achieve a life of confidence and strength, no matter what one faces. I am so fortunate to be able to learn from this brilliant woman."

Linda Solomon, photojournalist, author of
The Queen Next Door: Aretha Franklin, An Intimate Portrait
founder Pictures of Hope
member Michigan Journalism Hall of Fame

Oranges for Eve

My Brave,
Beautiful,
Badass
Journey to
the Feminine
Divine

BY RABBI TAMARA KOLTON PH.D.

ORANGES FOR EVE

My Brave, Beautiful, Badass Journey to the Feminine Divine

By Rabbi Tamara Kolton Ph.D.

Just Fly Publishing

74 W Long Lake Rd Suite 100

Bloomfield Hills, MI 48304

ISBN: 978-0-578-54036-8

Interior Formatting/Design by Transcendent Publishing

Cover Design by Elizabeth Mackey

Disclaimer: This book is memoir. It reflects the author's present recollections of experiences over time. Some names and characteristics have been changed, some events have been compressed, and some dialogue has been recreated.

Printed in the United States of America.

This book is dedicated to my children, Lior and Maya.

Being your mother is the greatest of all gifts. You are the two most extraordinary people I know. I respect you and adore you.

And to my husband, Isaac. Thank you for loving me and believing in me, always.

Yes. I would marry you all over again.

Contents

Acknowledgments   xi

Dear Soul Sister   xv

Introduction   1

The First Day: Because I Had to Follow My Truth   9

    July 2012   10

    The Temple   12

    "You're Gonna Need an Exit Story"   22

    Spiritual Exercise: *When Did You "Just Know"?*   26

The Second Day: The Yearning to Become a Butterfly   29

    The Spirit of Grandma Jeanette   30

    Rabbi Seeking Spiritual Home   34

    Skiing into the Spiritual Crevasse of Patriarchy   41

    Spiritual Exercise: What Is Your Butterfly Story?   47

The Third Day: The F*ing Fig Leaf   49

    In the Beginning… We Were Shamed   50

    What is a F*ing Fig Leaf?   52

    How Do You Wear Yours?   54

    Middle School and the Day I Forgot to Put My Bra On   58

    How Do We Heal?   60

    Spiritual Exercise: My F*ing Fig Leaf   77

The Fourth Day: Letting in the Light   79

    Coming Home to Yourself   80

    The Wounded Healer   82

    The Heroine's Journey   88

    Spiritual Exercise: Where Are You on Your Heroine's
    Journey?   93

**The Fifth Day: Remembering Who We Once Were with the
Mother God**   97

Hypnotized by Patriarchy 98
The Missing Queen of Heaven 106
The Seated Mother Goddess 110
Falling in Love with Catal Huyuk 113
The Virus of Patriarchy 123
Patriarchy: How the Hell Did It Happen? 126
God as a Woman Timeline: 128
Herstory/History Chart 129
Spiritual Exercise: Images of The Mother God 130
The Sixth Day: How to Access Great Mother Energy **139**
Meet the Great Mothers: An Interfaith Experience 140
Spiritual Exercise: Visiting with the Great Mothers 145
Into the Divine Sisterhood 149
Going Back with Great Mother Love 154
Becoming Your Own Great Mother 156
Spiritual Exercise: The Front Steps 158
Spiritual Exercise: Beautiful Baby 159
Spiritual Exercise: Becoming a Love Conductor 160
The Seventh Day: Life as a Free Bird **163**
The Spiritual Imperative of Our Time 164
Spiritual Exercise: A New Myth of Eve 168
On the Seventh Day… 169
Spiritual Exercise: Your Turn to Write a New Story
    of Creation 170
Today 171
Truth vs Lies: It's Apples to Oranges 176
Spiritual Exercise: YOU Are the Empowered Storyteller 178
My Empowered Story 179
References **181**
Keep Your Quest On! **183**
Contact **185**
About the Author **187**

Acknowledgments

T hank you, Mom. You are my North. Wherever I am, I calibrate to you. No one has been more influential in my life than you. No one has taught me more or loved me longer. You are my mother and my best friend.

Thank you, Dad. You raised me not as a girl, but as an equal citizen. As a physician for women's health, you walked the walk of a feminist. When I was a young child, you brought the sound of poetry and the love of the ocean into my life. Today, water and meter quench the thirst in my soul.

Thank you to my family. There is nowhere I would rather be than with you. When we are together my belly laughs and my heart sings. You are the sweetest nectar.

Thank you, Emily Heckman. You are an extraordinarily talented editor and a good friend. You were instrumental in giving this book its initial shape. Your gorgeous choice of words and passionate commitment to being kind can be felt throughout this book.

Thank you, Anne Doyle for "Powering Me Up!" You challenged me and encouraged me. Your careful, loving, chapter by chapter read of the manuscript elevated the content here and my spirit.

Thank you to every one of my friends. I treasure you.

Thank you, Lori Lipten. You provided me with an access point to the world beyond ordinary reality. You gave language to a paradigm for understanding life and death in an entirely different way. In connecting me to loved ones in spirit and helping me heal, it was as if you were applying spiritual balm directly to my chafed soul.

Thank you, Rabbi Sherwin T. Wine. You were in life—and still are in spirit—my greatest mentor and guiding force. You taught me to be strong and brave and remember that, "The joy is in the climbing." You taught me how to think through the world of ideas, even if we did not always arrive at the same conclusions. My love for you endures.

Thank you to the many people in the community who have given me the privilege to serve them as a rabbi. This includes the many incredible human beings I met through the Birmingham Temple during my years there. I thank you.

Finally, thank you to all the great women and men who came before me and who stand with me now in acknowledging the single, most urgent truth: <u>We are here on planet Earth to love.</u> Anything that does not support this truth is a lie.

Thank you, Truthtellers.

"If you have yet to be called an incorrigible, defiant woman, don't worry, there is still time."
~Clarissa Pinkola Estés

Eve Overcome by Remorse, Anna Lea Merritt, oil on canvas, 1885

**"Then the Lord God said to the woman,
'You will suffer terribly when you give birth.
But you will still desire your husband,
and he will rule over you.'"
~Genesis 3:16**

Dear Soul Sister,

In 2012, I experienced a spiritual crisis of epic proportion. I was then the senior rabbi of a temple near Detroit, Michigan, a job I adored in the same congregation I had grown up in. As a teenager, this temple gave me precious emotional sanctuary from the drama of my parents' marriage and, later, their divorce. Many times in my life, the temple was the only place where I felt at home. But once I turned forty, something changed. Suddenly, I found myself haunted by a deep sense of longing for something else, something more. I tried to ignore these feelings, but the Universe had a different plan. That July, I collided with the temple's board of directors in a crazy battle of wills that led to my resignation.

I lost my income and my pulpit; the doors to my beloved community were now literally locked behind me. Worst of all, I felt so ashamed. It was my equivalent to the fall from Paradise.

"I just wish you had left the temple with your dignity," said my mother. Yeah – me, too. But grace was not available to me then. We never fall into Grace. No. First, we hit the pavement.

I left because I had to follow my truth or I would have died inside.

Have you ever felt like that? Have you ever been compelled to do something drastic to save your spirit?

Through my pain, I felt as though a Divine message was trying to get through to me. What was this voice? To whom did it belong? Was it God calling to me? It was as if I could actually feel this force on my back like a hand pushing me forward, dislodging me and urging me to "Move on!"

I came to understand the force more as a feeling than a being. The feeling was definitely feminine in nature and was attached to a very old, very powerful story—a myth, really—of a woman named Eve. You know the one: Eve of the garden, the snake and the poisonous apple.

I could actually feel Eve's energy pulsating through me, like she was protesting, *"It isn't right! What you know about me isn't right! I am so much more. You deserve to know the truth. Women deserve the truth!"*

After my resignation, I set out on a quest to understand what I was feeling and what Eve was asking of me. I knew that I had to unlock the myth and free her, like freeing a genie trapped in a bottle buried deep inside the earth. What I would learn over the next seven years was that, in freeing Eve, I was freeing myself as well. What follows is my journey of self-discovery, empowerment and healing. It holds a bold message about truth, light and feminine power that has been burning inside me for years, aching to pour forth through my typing fingers to reach you.

Why? Because whenever women are shamed, silenced, opp-resssed, suppressed, self-doubting, approval-seeking, playing small or competing against rather than with one another, the world suffers from a lack of feminine light. But when a woman sets out on a quest to recover her lost light—to stand in her truth and refuse to believe the lies, the light of the Feminine Divine shines upon all of us.

For 2,000 years feminine power has been constricted, shut down, burned, slayed, hung on the gallows, covered up and exploited. Finally, the time has come to recover from this history. We are going to embark on a beautiful, brave, badass journey to unlock the vault the patriarchy used to seal up Eve's energy over 2,000 years ago. In opening Eve's vault, we will open all the vaults in our lives that lock away the truth of our Divinity.

This book is an invitation to be a *spiritual activist*!

The quest to find Eve, who is the embodiment of the lost feminine nature of God, is the quest to live our lives as Divine beings. Nothing less. This quest will nourish you, inspire you and heal you. It will give you real power to transform your life and the world, too.

So, take my hand, because together we are going to rise up out of the flames to become the free, brave birds that we were always each meant to be!

With all my love,

Tamara

September 2019

Introduction

Most of us know the myth of Adam and Eve, but for those who don't, here it is in a nutshell:

God creates Adam, but Adam is lonely. So God takes one of Adam's ribs and uses it to create Eve. Adam and Eve live in The Garden of Eden/Paradise, and it is FANTASTIC there! They are never in any pain and all their needs are met. With one exception: There is temptation. In the center of the garden is the Tree of Eternal Life. God explicitly instructs Adam and Eve *never* to eat from it. But Eve disobeys God. She picks the apple and takes a bite. She then gives the fruit to Adam, who eats it, too. Suddenly Eve is aware that she is naked and covers herself with a fig leaf. God is furious and His relationship with humankind is forever scarred by her sin.

So according to this myth, basically in less than five minutes, a woman destroys the world.

As punishment, God tells Eve:

> "I will make your pains in childbearing very severe;
> with painful labor you will give birth to your children.
> Your desire will be for your husband,
> and he will rule over you." (Genesis 3:16)

In the blink of an eye, Eve is cast outside of the garden, naked, stripped of everything of value—her spiritual power, her credibility, her joy, her body, her hope—all the bright gems that make a woman's life beautiful. She is forever cursed to be subordinate to

1

Adam, as all women will be to men. She will birth children in excruciating pain, as all women will. She will forever "long for her husband," meaning, she will want to have sex all the time (just in case you doubted that a man wrote the story).

Paradise is over. Eve ruined it for all of us and then... she vanishes. We never hear anything from Eve again. Adam goes on to beget Cain and Abel and all the generations of Noah. His story lives. But Eve? What becomes of Eve?

It was the greatest robbery of all time. Not only was everything taken from this supreme Goddess; she was disappeared from history. And the crime went unreported.

Until now.

"Hello. My name is Rabbi Tamara Kolton. I'm here to report a crime. Get me the best detectives you have!"

After years of soul searching I'm calling it like it is: a massive public flogging that would last for centuries. It was precedent-setting.

The story of Eve and her alleged crime would both fuel and justify violence against women in all forms and in all societies for the next two millennia. This brutality includes the unrecorded murders of thousands of women killed for two crimes: disobedience and use of spiritual power.

Between 1692 and 1693, twenty people, mostly women, were tortured and executed in Salem, Massachusetts for practicing witchcraft. While most of us have heard of the Salem witch trials, we have no concept of the depth and breadth of violence against women in the Western world. We don't realize that in the three hundred years prior to Salem, *tens of thousands* of women were executed for being "witches." Why? Because we leave these women outside of history. Just like Eve.

The Myth of Eve, as it is written in Genesis and as it has been perpetuated for the last 2,000 years, is a lie of criminal proportion. This lie drained women of their power and their birthright to live as Divine beings.

This lie claims that not only was Eve a sinner, but she *brought*

2

sin into the world. Yes, Adam, too, was punished. <u>But Eve was blamed.</u> The patriarchy claimed that she disobeyed God and ruined Paradise for everyone, especially men. They claimed that she was dangerous and could not be trusted. For this, she deserved to be punished and needed to be silenced. They wrote all this down in the Bible and said it was the Word of God.

Then, down through the generations, came the rest of us, all saddled to one degree or another with the burden of being descendants of this sneaky, duplicitous woman and presumably capable of similar crimes. Like Eve, we were blamed and considered poisonous, so they didn't let us vote and they certainly didn't let us lead. They preferred us to be pretty and pretty silent. But over the years, we began to make progress! We got the vote and control over our bodies; more of us rose through the corporate ranks and became financially independent. And, not too long ago, in the United States, we were sure that we were finally going to have a woman president. Instead of her, on November 8, 2016, Americans elected as their president a misogynist and a liar.

Why?

Because his opponent – a woman – was just too dangerous. *She* could not be trusted. Just like Eve, she needed to be silenced and punished. We were reasonably comfortable with *his* secrecy – the fact that he would not share his tax returns or that he used bankruptcy as a way to get richer. Americans were even okay with his misogynistic language and behavior. On the other hand, Hillary Clinton's improper behavior, particularly around her money and her email accounts, resulted in her being deemed "poisonous." She had unknowingly activated a pandemic of poisonous Eve mythology. Indeed, many Trump supporters—including white women—were not voting *for* him as much as they were voting *against* her.

At that point, it had been about 2,463 years from the time the Bible was canonized with the myth of Eve, yet it was as if no time had passed. The lie was that pervasive, that penetrating, that contaminating.

To be clear, this is *not* about Republicans or Democrats. It's not about whether or not you like Trump or think Hillary Clinton would have made a better president. *It's much, much bigger than that.*

This is not about politics.
It's about awakening to truth.

Truth: It is time for women to learn *how* to stand together and support each other. Our destinies are inextricably bound together. Imagine our power! Nothing has the power to heal like women working in dedicated, loving, and kind collaboration with one another. And this, in and of itself, is a pretty radical truth for many women to embrace.

After I resigned from my temple and began the process of redefining my spiritual life, I began to wonder... What if being banished from Paradise wasn't the end of Eve's story, but *the beginning* of it? What if WE decided it is time to rescue her from oblivion and reconnect with her so we might be able to fulfill our own spiritual potential? What if reconnecting with Eve could heal us as women and restore our essential power? What if we were finally able to see the truth and free ourselves from all the lies that have been foisted upon us that shame us and silence us?

"Listen to the silence
It has so much to say."
~Rumi

These questions led to more questions: What if Eve wasn't who they said she was? If the authors of the Bible found her so threatening that she needed to be silenced, what was she saying that was so "dangerous?" Maybe Eve represented an opposing viewpoint to patriarchy?

Could we restore the energetic connection
between ourselves and the Feminine Divine?

What if we, as women today, *could* talk to God, in the way that *we* understand God?

Could we retie the silken thread?

Over the past seven years, I've asked myself those questions in a thousand different ways. At times, I felt like I was talking to Eve and she was showing me. I believe that her spirit compelled me to write this book and tell her story. I believe just as strongly that she is asking you to tell her story, too.

It is a story that up until just a few years ago I really knew nothing about. There I was, a middle-aged feminist living in modern-day America with internet access and an Amazon account, yet I never knew the truth about the deep roots of feminine spiritual power.

I had no idea that prior to 3,000 years ago, and going back at least 25,000 years before that, men and women believed the earth was the sacred womb of The Great Mother and *shared* spiritual, social and political power. I was turned off by terms like "pagan," "witch," "New Age," and even "Goddess." I thought pagans were unsophisticated people who worshipped "stuff"; witches did scary shit in the woods; and New Age thinking was made up by people on hallucinogens. And Goddesses? Well, they were just fake Gods with boobs.

My myopia is not that surprising, considering I did not have a single role model for how to have a full spiritual life in relationship to the Feminine Divine. I knew about some of the recent archae-ological discoveries in Israel that proved how pagan the Israelites really were, but it never even occurred to me that their idols, far from being just "fertility figures," were actually how our ancestors imagined God in the female form. I certainly did not know how peaceful the women-oriented societies were. Crete, for example, was war-free for a thousand years. Similarly, Catal Huyuk, a city located in present-day Turkey, knew no violence for eighteen hundred years. Its people shared power equally between women and men and enjoyed a rich spiritual life that revolved around the Great Mother. Sound too good to be true? Just wait. I'm going to show you the undeniable archaeological evidence that has surfaced in the last 150 years.

So how did we go from those kinds of societies to the world we live in today?

In 1976, Merlin Stone published the groundbreaking book, *When God Was A Woman,* in which she posed the question:

> How did it actually happen? How did men initially gain the control that now allows them to regulate the world in matters so vastly diverse as deciding which wars will be fought when to what time dinner should be served?

Indeed, I asked myself after reading Stone's work, *how the hell did that happen?* What had changed to tip the balance of power in men's favor, to shift from a reverence of the feminine body and spirit dating back to Paleolithic times to the misogyny that continues today? It was a concept I had never considered before; I'd just assumed men had always been in charge.

"My name is Rabbi Tamara Kolton and I am here to report a crime. Half of our stories have gone missing."

The myth of Eve is the story of stories; because through her story all other stories can be told.

Contrary to what they would have us believe, Eve did not disappear. She did not die. She is alive and well and living through you and me every time we choose hope over despair, every time we fight for self-worth and especially when we support this energy in other women. Eve is a living force of energy that flows through us, leading us back to Source. We are not meant to live in shame. We are meant to be held in the bosom of our Divine Mother and share our light with all living beings.

Eve is the connective tissue between the patriarchal world that took hold approximately 2,000 years ago and the matriarchal world that extends at least 25,000 years before. She is the epic clue to what was lost and how it was taken. Most of all, Eve is a living field of

6

Cosmic Mother Energy that is the missing spiritual home so many of us are seeking. I'm going to teach you all about that. This book is a spiritual recovery program.

Eve is the crown jewel and the scepter for you to carry on your quest to reclaim your own Divinity.

In this book, we are going to celebrate the very qualities Eve was punished for – disobedience, spiritual power, and self-esteem! *Oranges for Eve* is organized into seven chapters to mirror the story of the seven days of Creation in Genesis. I've included stories of some of the most radiant women who broke free from the poisonous apples they were forced to swallow as children, young women and even into old age. After each new day, there is a spiritual exercise to engage you in new learning. You can write in this book or use a journal to work alongside it. The exercises are all yummy, loving, and deeply nourishing.

With each new chapter, you will be able to feel less shame and guilt, less sadness, and more joy. With each chapter, you will feel more and more powerful and Divinely supported. This is a new story which will uplift you, nourish you and fill you with love.

Why the title *Oranges for Eve*? Because we are done eating poisonous apples; we are done perpetuating the old lies. We are writing a new story. It's the story of a woman's *re-creation*.

This time, instead of being silenced, we will be encouraged to be brave, disobedient and love ourselves and each other as the image of God. This new creation story uplifts us and rewards us for pushing patriarchal boundaries and challenging misogynistic mythology, even if it comes to us from the Bible.

You could say, *it's apples to oranges.*

The orange is also a symbol in the movement for Jewish women to have religious authority equal to men. The urban legend goes like this: Several years ago, an orthodox rabbi remarked that a woman belongs on the *bima* (stage or altar) like an orange belongs on a Seder plate. What he meant was—she *doesn't* belong. As an act of resistance, progressive Jewish households began to put oranges on their Seder plates. Today at Seders all over the world, the orange sits alongside matzah to represent the fact that, yes, women do belong on the bima. So it feels perfect to me that we offer this golden gift of reverence to our one true spiritual mother, the one who was forcibly taken from us so long ago. Eve deserves so much better— as do you, as do I, as do we all.

As my good friend Ruth, an expert in handwriting, says, "When the story of your life is written, make sure that you are the one holding the pen."

Well… ladies, we are taking back the pen! The time has come for us to write our own stories. Now, it is now up to us to decide who and what we are. And what we have to say is BIG and (speaking of apples) pretty damn golden delicious!

Oranges for Eve is a manifesto of feminine spiritual truth. We are going to take on all the lies that limit our power and steal our joy. We are going to name and then break free from the paradigms that constrict us, because Eve was no sinner. Eve was the first one to have the audacity to act on her own behalf. Eve was being true to herself. That is why she picked the apple. Eve did not bring sin into the world. She brought truth and spiritual bravery.

Eve was a badass.

So are you.

The First Day

Because I Had to Follow My Truth

Expulsion from Paradise, Michelangelo, Sistine Chapel, Painted 1508-1512

*"One day you finally knew
what you had to do and began,
though the voices around you
kept shouting their bad advice—
though the whole house
began to tremble..."*
~The Journey, Mary Oliver

July 2012

"You're going to regret this," the temple board member hisses in my ear. Her hiss is meant to threaten and silence me. She wasn't always a snake. For many years I considered her a role model, a friend even. But tonight, at this emergency meeting of our temple board, it's become clear: I have no more friends.

This moment had been coming for some time, yet I am still blindsided by it. At issue is whether I am "fit" to continue serving as the rabbi, a role I was chosen for by the temple's beloved founder. I've been the senior rabbi for eight years now, and during that time I've married these people, buried their loved ones, blessed their newborns, Bar and Bat Mitzvahed their children and broken bread with them. But now none of that seems to matter; all I'm feeling from them, my spiritual family, my community, is raw, un-adulterated *hatred*. The air is so thick with it that my face burns, my ears buzz. It feels as though my heart is being tasered. It is brutal.

It also ignites in me the instinct to fight back and with such force that even I—who have never been a shrinking violet—am surprised. It went something like this:

"Why can't you just move on, Rabbi Kolton? Why do you insist on talking about this? You just keep bringing it up and bringing it up!"

"I need an apology," I insist.

The board member glares back at me, pointing his finger. "You are *not* going to get an apology."

"Then I *can't* move on."

I grit my teeth, lower my eyes like a bull, and get ready to draw blood when suddenly the building custodian comes in and tells me that I need to check on my car. When I get to the parking lot, there is broken glass everywhere. Every window of my minivan has been smashed in. I run to the car and look in to see my wallet lying on the passenger seat, untouched. My daughter's car seat and stuffed animals are still in the backseat. The police come and walk around the car, shaking their heads. Since nothing has been taken, they determine it's an act of aggression. On the police report the officer checks the "vandalism" box, then writes the word "attack."

We are fighting about money. I've been raising a stink because I believe that the board has not been transparent about funds. But what's really happening is so much bigger than that.

Two days before the meeting I had gotten a call from my mother, and a taste of the ugliness to come.

"Tammy. It's Mom," she said when I picked up the phone. "You're not going to like what I'm about to tell you, but just listen."

My stomach dropped.

"The chairman of the temple called. He's said that he's worried about you. He told me he thinks you've become mentally unstable. "He called the police to the temple today to report that you were stealing checks from the office."

Her words quite literally knocked the wind out of me. It's as if I'm suddenly back in elementary school gym class, playing dodge ball, and I've been hit in the stomach by the rubber ball so hard I can't breathe. I gasped so loudly that Maya, my seven-year old, heard, ran into the room and grabbed me around the waist. Sounds I didn't even know I could make came out of me and, with Maya still glued to my side, I went into the bathroom and tried to keep from hyperventilating. Of all the things I might be accused of.... stealing? *Me?* The person who will run to return a dollar bill blowing down an empty street? Rationally, I knew I hadn't done anything wrong, yet I felt something familiar and awful. What was it? Embarrassment? No, not embarrassment. And then I realized what it was: I felt humiliated.

I managed to ask my mother, "Was there something missing?"

"No," she said, "They couldn't even file a police report because there was nothing to write about."

Earlier that day, I had been at the office rifling around, looking for a check: *my missing paycheck.* Isaac, my Israel-born husband, insisted we go down there and get what was rightfully mine. Never mind that we needed the money for groceries, he wanted me to do it on principal. While we were there, we were talking in Hebrew and we were loud. I railed about the crazy bunch of bullies who were determined to run the temple into the ground. And what liars they were! Isaac, in his booming voice, egged me on.

The only person in the building at the time was a secretary I didn't know very well. I saw her there but it never occurred to me that there was any problem, other than her hearing me at my Hebrew loudest. I had no idea that the whole thing was about to go down old school KGB-style.

Apparently, she called the board officers, who then called the police to report a robbery in progress in the temple office. The suspect? The rabbi. For weeks afterward, my husband walked around our house shaking his head and humorously trying to lighten the mood by saying, (in his thick Israeli accent) "I tink zis is za first time in za history of za Jewish people zat za police were called on da rabbi!"

How had it come to this? How had the place that had been my life-long sanctuary become so dangerous to me? *How had I become so dangerous to it?*

The Temple

In 1963 a liberal progressive Jewish temple was founded in the suburbs of Detroit. Actually, the words *liberal* and *progressive* might not totally capture the place. I would include "Radical" with a capital "R" and "edgy"—like so edgy if it were any edgier it would fall off the cliff of the Jewish world.

Its founder, Reform Rabbi Sherwin T. Wine, was a bold, brilliant visionary who had grown up in a kosher home. Rabbi Wine was a true genius. He not only knew the history of EVERYTHING, but he had a photographic memory. During my rabbinic training, I sat in when he met with families to prepare for a funeral. Imagine a two-hour meeting with ten people all telling their stories about someone Rabbi Wine had never met. He would sit there listening, never taking a single note. Two days later, Rabbi Wine would stand up at the service and give a thirty-minute eulogy, integrating every detail of what he had heard with fabulous anecdotes and moving stories.

"How do you do that?" I asked him one day as we walked out from a funeral service.

"Well," he replied, "you have categories in your mind and you put the information you hear into those categories to organize your thinking."

"Oh," I remember saying respectfully, but thinking to myself, *like huh?* His mind was like a data bank, full of volumes of information he was able to synthesize in such a way that when he spoke his words dazzled like diamonds. He was also very funny. He mocked his opponents, poked holes in their theories and made fun of the absurdities of life. His energy was infectious, and it was not uncommon to hear people roaring with laughter during his sermons. To his followers, he was a superstar.

Although he did not speak about it often, he was also a gay man. This, in addition to his radical views, made him a double outsider in the Jewish community of his day.

As a young man, he broke ranks with Reform Judaism to found a sect built around his belief that you could practice Judaism without believing in God. He called this movement Humanistic Judaism: a philosophy of life that affirms that the message of Jewish history is that the Jews survived because of human qualities—not because of God. Rabbi Wine believed that God did not choose the Jews, and He certainly did not save them. Furthermore, he taught that it was demeaning to worship such a God. He explained, "If I managed a company the way God manages the Universe, I'd be fired." So, Rabbi Wine did what no one else seemed to have the guts to do: he fired God.

In 1965, he was featured in *Time* magazine. "I find no adequate reason to accept the existence of a supreme person," he stated in the article. That same year, in an interview with *The San Diego Jewish Journal,* he said, "The message of the Holocaust is that there isn't any magic power."

In his temple, he believed in celebrating all the Jewish holidays and passages of life, but disavowed worship. The word "meditation" replaced the word "prayer" and the traditional vocabulary for spirituality was refocused on personal development. In his most radical move of all, Rabbi Wine decided to take the Torah, the holiest scroll that has been carried in the arms of the Jewish people for 2,000 years, out of the Temple Arc and move it to the library. He did this because he considered the Torah to be no holier than any other book. Decades later, this was still controversial. I remember when I was on a panel representing the different Jewish movements in Detroit. A woman stood up, pointed at me and said, "I have a question for *that* rabbi, "Is it true that Rabbi Wine keeps the Torah in his desk drawer?"

Well, not quite, but…close.

In the late 70s my parents joined the temple, after hearing about it from my mother's best friend. They knew it was radical and they took flak from other Jews in the community, but the secularism appealed to them and they found the services, which were in English, to be very meaningful. The year I turned seven, my older brother Jason and I were enrolled in Sunday School.

Jason hated everything about the place. He was intimidated by Rabbi Wine and he didn't think that Rabbi Wine liked him much either. Along with his best friend Michael, he made so much trouble in Hebrew class that Rabbi Wine frequently asked "Yaakov" and "Menachem" (my brother and Michael's Hebrew names, respectively) to please "excuse themselves."

There was no denying that Rabbi Wine could be tough. Every class began the same way: "Take off your jacket, spit out your gum and where are your books?" If you didn't have them, he would ask you in his booming voice, "And what is the reason you do not have your books?" Then he would go around the library table, asking the same question to any child spotted without books.

How were we supposed to know where our books were? At our father's apartment? At our mom's house? In the back of the carpool station wagon? It was the late seventies and early eighties. Everyone was getting divorced. In creative custody arrangements, our shit was all over the place. A shotgun-second after his Bar-Mitzvah, my brother headed for the hills. I, however, took to the place like a duck to water.

When a Jewish child is thirteen, they experience a ritual marking their passage into adulthood. The entire community gathers together as the child becomes a teacher of Torah. The Bar Mitzvah (for a boy) or Bat Mitzvah (for a girl) literally means, "son or daughter of the commandment" and this is marked by a ceremonial reading of the Torah.

At our temple, instead of reading from the Torah, students chose a hero to research and on the day of the ceremony, the students shared with the rest of the congregation what they'd learned about their chosen hero. We were encouraged to choose someone who was Jewish and/or a Humanist. Over the years, a few kids pushed the boundaries and chose great change-makers like Martin Luther King and Gandhi. (One kid chose Moses and this was considered almost heresy.) Every once in a while, a family would insist on reading from the Torah, and when this happened, Rabbi Wine would select a passage he felt wasn't too offensive and have it photocopied onto a sheet of paper. The Torah scroll would stay in the library. The talk around town was that these were not "real" Bar-Mitzvahs and our friends teased us that all we were doing were book reports.

For his hero, my brother chose Jessie Steinfeld, the Surgeon General who successfully changed cigarette packaging labels to include health warnings. For months, my brother walked around our modern suburban house, repeatedly and somewhat obnoxiously announcing, "Warning: The Surgeon General has determined that cigarette smoking is dangerous to your health!" I think he chose Steinfeld because he wanted to drive my mom crazy enough to stop smoking (which she later did).

I chose Eleanor Roosevelt as my Bat Mitzvah heroine. I chose her not only because she was a great humanitarian, but because she described feeling like the "ugly duckling" in her family—a duckling who grew up to become one of the most powerful, loving, and empowered human beings on earth. I wanted to be like her. I wanted to help people in big ways and to feel empowered too. And when I looked out at the congregation on the day of my Bat Mitzvah, I felt a surge of personal power and love that catapulted me past all my fears and anxieties. I was on top of the world. On the day of my Bat Mitzvah I fell in love for the first time: with the temple and the Jewish people.

On that day, at age thirteen, I decided, "I'm going to be a Humanistic rabbi!"

It's not like I drank the Kool-Aid without ever asking *any* questions. As a teenager, I bravely and somewhat pridefully posed to Rabbi Wine, "What do you think happens when people die?"

"You rot," he replied, and then, because I probably looked shocked, he added, "And you live on in the lives of the people you touched."

On another occasion I asked, "How can you ever know *for sure* that there's no God?" He smiled and answered, "Truth is based on experience and evidence. I have no experience of a deity and the history of the Jews is evidence that there is no God available to us."

Okay. I partially agreed, so I settled on being an agnostic, a person who takes the philosophical position of not knowing. Given the choice between believing in a manmade God and denying any possibility of a higher power, *not knowing* felt right; it was also an acceptable position for humanists. It never occurred to me that there were many more options than this limited menu, including the possibility of a Feminine Divine. Even if I had been looking for something else in those early years, I wouldn't have known what I was looking for. It would have been like chasing the darkness.

Years later, I began formulating different ideas about God. One night before bed I declared to Isaac, "I believe God is an energy field."

He looked up at me and asked, "You are going to stand up in front of people at the temple and tell them that you believe in energy?"

"Yes," I asserted, to which Isaac responded, "Good luck with that."

Most kids dropped out of temple school after their Bar or Bat Mitzvahs, and by ninth grade there were only five or six of us left in class. Sometimes only one or two would show up. This meant that for my entire adolescence, I had an almost private tutorial in philosophy and the Jewish people with Rabbi Wine. He taught me how to think and how to look at the world as an outsider, a skeptic, and a Jew. He was enthusiastic, charismatic, and fully alive. Yes, he could be intimidating—very intimidating—but he could also be soft and exceptionally kind.

There were countless times over the years when I sought him out to help me cope with my life. No matter how busy he was, he left his office door cracked open, and when I appeared there he'd put aside whatever he was working on and warmly invite me in. His counsel empowered me to dig deep and find the courage and strength to live my life with dignity. When I shared how ashamed I felt about being overweight, he replied, "In my eyes, you are radiant." When he said this, I felt what every young woman yearns to feel: I felt pretty. I felt special. Most of all, I felt safe. Truly, the temple was the only place I felt safe in my life. I was so grateful to be there, to be within the walls of the Eden Rabbi Wine had created.

In 1999, after seven years of study, including a Ph.D., I became the first person to be ordained a Humanistic rabbi. By then Rabbi Wine was approaching retirement and the temple had started searching for his successor. I enviously watched candidates going into their meetings with the search committee, and each time the door opened I wanted to jump up and shout, "Me! I'm over here!" But no one even considered me. I was in my twenties and the people on the search committee had known me since I was a child. They just didn't see me as a rabbi, let alone *their* rabbi. I mean, how could a five-foot-tall young woman fill such a giant's shoes?

Indeed, it seemed no one could fill Rabbi Wine's shoes. For years, the interviewing process continued, and the reports from the grapevine sounded like a bad date: "I just didn't feel the chemistry," or "I just can't see a future with him." Meanwhile, I steadily made my way up the ranks and proved myself as Rabbi Wine's assistant. I counseled, taught, and gave sermons—all the while keeping my eye on the prize. As time went on, a fierce competition among rabbi hopefuls broke out. At this point, we were less like *Humanistic* Jews and more like a pack of pit bulls straining on their chains. I played hard. I fought hard. I worked hard. And after ten years of throwing my elbows around with the best of them, I finally got the job.

Being the temple rabbi was the best job in the world. My life was jam-packed with meaning. A typical weekend wasn't so much "Four Weddings and A Funeral" as it was, "Two weddings, a Bar-Mitzvah, a baby-naming and a funeral."

My brother joked, "My sister: has *chupa* (wedding canopy), will travel." He also named me "Miss Jamaica" because I was always on the move, running around town with a million different jobs, which is apparently what people do in Jamaica to make ends meet.

Each week, I looked forward to Friday evening, when the moon rose and we welcomed the Shabbat. Every single Friday, come Midwest snowstorm or high water—I shared Shabbat with my temple family. Sometimes twenty people showed up for services and sometimes two hundred. It didn't seem to matter. Shabbat always brought a feeling of pure radiance into my week and illuminated my life like the dancing twin flames of the candles themselves.

Over time, the bonds I formed with temple members, adults and children, were tied tight with sacred connections. It was a gorgeous, intricate web laced together in hospitals, cemeteries, the Sunday school and around the Seder table. We laughed together, sang together, studied together and we cried together for years and years. As a rabbi, I lit thousands of candles with people for thousands of reasons. And every spark flew straight to my heart.

I can say emphatically that ninety percent of my experiences with the people of the temple were overwhelmingly positive; they were blessings. The temple gave me the greatest of all gifts—to walk with people on the best and worst days of their lives. I believe the vast majority of the temple members felt the same; some of them even became dear, cherished friends. Together, we were flying over the moon. But ten percent of people can make for a lot of disruption and quite a crash landing.

There was a group of temple members who never thought I should have been chosen as Rabbi Wine's successor. And there were a few others who just didn't like me or who, at some point in time, stopped liking me. I made mistakes. Never intentionally, but I made them. Sometimes I knew when I made a mistake, and other times I had absolutely no idea what went wrong.

My rabbinate was peppered by several "showdowns." *Just hang in there,* I'd tell myself. *In the end, you'll be the one to turn off the lights.* I felt like my job was a game of Survivor. I had to outwit, outplay, and outlast. For example, there was the day that Rabbi Wine held in his hand a letter, written by a half-dozen people declaring they had no confidence in Tamara Kolton as the rabbi of the temple. This came as a complete shock to me.

"Why didn't you tell me?" I pleaded to Rabbi Wine. What I really wanted to know was, *Why aren't you defending me?* A while later a different letter, unsigned and without a return address, was sent via snail mail to a select group of people. Over the next several months, this same letter, which contained a laundry list of complaints about me, would arrive each week.

When I got my hands on a copy—a two-pager, no less—I sat at my desk, thinking hard about whether or not to read it. In the end I decided to crumple it up and throw it in the garbage; yet, even unread, it hurt. *What was going on? Was this normal for a rabbi?* I pleaded with Rabbi Wine to have my back. He listened. He sympathized. But he never did anything. In fact, he continued to allow the disgruntled to come to him, complain, and organize negative campaigns.

The connecting thread between each and every person who gave me a hard time or tried to sabotage me was an intense attachment to Rabbi Wine. I would even say it was an irrational attachment to him. What was going on? What was *really* going on? The truth is that we were, consciously or unconsciously, all playing a zero-sum game in a competition for Rabbi Wine's love. This is a daring truth, considering that there were women and men who were actually *in love* with him, and women and men, who, like me, looked to him to fill a deep, primal void for unconditional parental love. It was a perfect psychological shitstorm.

Rationally, I knew that the vast majority of temple members loved and respected me. But I was so damn sensitive. And another thing: at some very deep level, I believed that the people who said I was bad were right. So I ate their poisonous apples. And I felt sick.

In the spring of 2007, I'd had enough. I finally stood up to Rabbi Wine and said, "In allowing this to go on, you are actually undermining your own legacy!" Saying this to him made me shake. He scowled and looked offended by my disrespect. The conversation ended without resolution, and we didn't talk much for the next several months. Then, the day before he left for his annual summer abroad, I received a voicemail from him: "Tamara, I'm off to Morocco. I'm sure you'll do a great job this summer. See you soon. All my love." The message sounded like he didn't want to leave for the entire summer with so much tension between us.

On July 21, 2007 at approximately 1 a.m., after an evening of theatre and a late dinner in a small Moroccan town, Rabbi Wine's taxi was hit by a drunk driver and he was killed. The New York Times article read:

"Sherwin Wine, 79, Founder of Splinter Judaism Group, Dies:

Rabbi Sherwin T. Wine, founder of a movement in Judaism that says there is no reason to believe in God but that the religion's highest ethical traditions and the value of each person should be revered, died on Saturday in Essaouira, Morocco."

His death would change my life forever. But not in the way that I ever could have imagined.

Two days after Rabbi Wine died, Lori came to see me. Lori is a shamanic medium who, like me, grew up at the temple. When she arrived, I was locked away in my office—the same office that had been Rabbi Wine's for forty years—intensely engaged in making his funeral arrangements.

"I hope it's okay that I just showed up here," Lori said, "I know you're busy but I really felt that I needed to see you."

I nodded, and we sat down in the chic leather club chairs beside my desk. "I know this might seem strange," she began, "and I do not want to do anything to disrespect your beliefs or boundaries. But I have a message for you from Spirit. Do I have your permission to relay it to you?"

"Yes!" I blurted out, although I didn't quite get what she was talking about. Lori began. "It's from Rabbi Wine. The rabbi is saying, 'I'm sorry. I failed you.' Do you know what he's talking about?" I knew. I felt his words go right to my soul, soothing it like a sacred balm.

"He wants me to tell you that he loves you," Lori continued. He says you are like the daughter he never had."

Now I was sobbing. Lori was sobbing. We sobbed together for a while and then she continued speaking Rabbi Wine's words: "'I didn't always understand you. I didn't know how to value your way of knowing. I didn't see you the way I should have. I see you now.'" Then she added, "The rabbi is saying three times, 'Thank you. Thank you. Thank you.' Actually, he is singing this to you."

I looked at her in astonishment. At his retirement, I'd sung a Natalie Merchant song to Rabbi Wine that began and ended with "thank you, thank you, thank you." Now he was singing it back to me.

It wasn't that Lori couldn't have known this. It wasn't beyond the realm of possibility that she was making it all up. But I knew she wasn't. I *knew* this was Rabbi Wine speaking to me. Nothing like this had ever happened to me before. Though Lori's voice was hers, she was channeling my mentor, my spiritual father, in real time.

I wanted to ask him some questions, and I did. Who should speak at his funeral? Was he okay? Did he know how deeply and fiercely I loved him and would always love him? This conversation could have lasted an hour or a thousand hours: It was beyond all time. It dislodged all the hurt and confusion from my heart in a way that a thousand therapy sessions never could. It liberated me and opened me to the next chapter in my life. Well, not just a chapter…

"You're Gonna Need an Exit Story"

At forty-two years old, I had lived almost all of my life as a Humanistic Jew. I had spent literally thousands of hours sitting at the big table in the temple's library. I had learned my best lessons there, taught there, eaten countless lunches there. Now I would resign there. This was it. I was walking away from the temple, my pulpit and my home.

It is 10:30 p.m. and the board members are outraged. One in particular wants to shoot me dead. I'm not exaggerating. He is yelling at me from the corner of the room, "You are an outrageous woman!" I am terrified but I don't show it. Instead, I exit the meeting, go into my office and sit down to write my letter of resignation. One of my allies follows me into my office.

"Oh, you're gonna need an exit story!" he says, and leans against my desk. I know what he means. I have to find my own narrative. *What will I say when people ask me why I left the temple?* Most of the members are totally oblivious that any of this drama is going on. *How will I explain not only why I left the temple, but Humanistic Judaism, too?* Was I leaving because they called the police on me? Was it because the management of the temple was so dysfunctional? Was I just sick of fighting? Maybe I wasn't strong enough? Or was it something else, something I guarded so close to my heart that I barely knew it myself?

There was an overwhelming feeling that although I felt utterly alone on an emotional level, I was not alone spiritually. I felt the presence of a force. The best way to describe it is to say it was like a hand on the small of my back—a strong hand pushing me forward to "Go!" There was a knowing deep inside my gut that I had to leave the temple, follow my truth and be brave. Very, very brave. If the force had words, it would have said: *You must leave. You are not meant to stay here any longer. You must be daring. Dare to follow your new path. Dare to save your life. Do not listen to them. Dare to listen to yourself.*

Although the circumstances around why I was leaving seemed wrong, the outcome was absolutely right. It was even necessary. Though the drama and the hatred would wound me more than I could predict, I felt as though I was being freed after being pinned under a huge rock. I was being dislodged from everything I'd ever known and it felt like I was being compelled, actually pushed forward in my life, by forces far greater than I or anyone in that late-night board room.

That's not to say I wasn't terrified. I was. Everything was on the line. But I also felt, however faintly, a whisper of hope that this was the only way I was going to move toward God. I was moving toward the great unknown; in fact, I was hurtling toward it. That same, strong current of energy that had told me I had to leave the temple was still there. It was a presence, an essence of something I'd been missing all my life. It was a force of love, feminine grace, power, bravery—and its name was Eve.

Of course, I didn't know this at that time. And I wouldn't be able to know it for some time to come.

That night marked my leaving my own Garden of Eden under the most confusing, devastating, and painful circumstances. I knew where I no longer belonged but I did not have any place to go. Up ahead were endless miles of wilderness, a vast emptiness that took my breath away.

By midnight I had no salary and my family had no health insurance. I had no idea how or where I would find a new job.

My very best friend from the temple now shunned me. She stopped returning my calls and never spoke to me again.

The next day I rented a crappy car to use while the windows of my minivan were being fixed. The rental car smelled terrible but it had a CD in it left by the previous user, and when I turned the car on I heard the familiar voices of Fleetwood Mac belting out, "Been down one time. Been down two times. I'm never going back again." I played that song hard while I drove that crappy rental car, singing, banging on the steering wheel to the banjo, crying, and trying so hard to release the shame and the pain, all the while thinking, *how am I going to live through this?*

As a final goodbye, a group of families and their children peti-tioned the board to give me a sendoff party. The board voted no, but the temple families threw me a party anyway. The building overflowed with love. I cried from the moment I stepped inside and I didn't even try to stop. It was as though a spigot opened and my tears just flowed and flowed and flowed. I was done pretending. I was finally on the road to being me without apologizing for my emotions.

In one of the most beautiful and tender moments of my life a little blue-eyed boy looked up at me and said, "I'm sure going to miss you."

I stayed until the last person left and then felt suddenly…alone. The only people still in the building were the custodian and my daughter Maya. I looked at her standing there, wearing white tights and black patent leather shoes, so little and so beautiful. She was now the same age as I was when I first walked into the temple thirty-five years earlier. With the surf of my life spread before me, I slowly made my way to her, wading through the waist-deep water of the unknown.

She was tired and ready to go home. "Mommy, it's time to kiss the temple goodbye," she said.

Together we pushed open the big wooden entrance doors and stepped outside into the cold Michigan air. We turned around and blew our kisses into the building as the big doors slowly closed on their old hinges. And with that, the last gate of a place that had once been my Eden locked behind me.

The Journey, By Mary Oliver

*One day you finally knew
what you had to do, and began,
though the voices around you
kept shouting
their bad advice –
though the whole house
began to tremble
and you felt the old tug
at your ankles.
"Mend my life!"
each voice cried.
But you didn't stop.
You knew what you had to do,
though the wind pried
with its stiff fingers
at the very foundations,
though their melancholy
was terrible.
It was already late
enough, and a wild night,
and the road full of fallen
branches and stones.
But little by little,
as you left their voices behind,
the stars began to burn
through the sheets of clouds,
and there was a new voice
which you slowly
recognized as your own,
that kept you company
as you strode deeper and deeper
into the world,
determined to do
the only thing you could do –
determined to save
the only life you could save.*

Spiritual Exercise

When Did You "Just Know"?

First, read Mary Oliver's poem, The Journey. Then continue to this meditation.

Take three deep, full, cleansing breaths. Allow yourself to drop down from your head, to your throat, to your heart, sliding down, down, down and landing on the safe floor of your gut. Feel what your gut feels like from the inside. Feel your diaphragm fill up from the inside. Is it tight or relaxed? Constricted or expansive? Become aware of the "You" inside of you—how you experience the world in the depth of your gut. Your gut is the seat of a great source of knowing. It's near your belly button which was how you were connected to your first physical source of nourishment. The mind talks us into things and out of things. But the gut *just knows.*

When did you just know? Maybe you knew you had to leave a relationship or a job, or begin one? Maybe you had to make a high-stakes decision or take a huge mental leap to believe something new about yourself?

Did the "whole house tremble," like in the poem? Did people "shout their bad advice" and, if they did, what was it they said? Did you heed their advice or did you "disobey"? Did you act on what you knew right away, or ever?

Consider also, what do you "just know" right now, in this moment?

Today I Just Know:

_____

_____

_____

_____

_____

_____

_____

_____

_____

_____

_____

_____

_____

_____

_____

_____

_____

_____

_____

_____

_____

_____

_____

_____

_____

_____

_____

_____

_____

_____

_____

_____

_____

_____

_____

_____

_____

_____

_____

_____

_____

_____

_____

_____

_____

_____

_____

_____

_____

_____

_____

_____

_____

_____

After you've written this down, take a few deep breaths. Honor what you wrote down. This is Eve calling to you. This is your heart's yearning and deep desire. Amen. Namaste. Shalom.

The Second Day

The Yearning to Become a Butterfly

Me and My Grandma Jeanette, 1993

*"Just when the caterpillar thought
the world was over,
it became a butterfly."*
~Proverb

The Spirit of Grandma Jeanette

In the days following my resignation, getting out of bed in the morning was nearly impossible. Everything hurt. My head hurt, my heart hurt, my ego hurt. Every cell in my body and every centimeter of my skin registered pain. I felt like someone had taken an ice cream scooper and scooped out my insides, exposing my guts for all the world to see. If I moved, I might start bleeding all over the place. If not for the blessing of having a young child who needed me, I think I would have spent those first few months sequestered in my bedroom.

Each morning Maya would come in, take her tiny foot and push me to the edge of the bed. "Come on, Mom! You have to get up!" She would then proceed to shove me until she literally kicked me out of bed.

"I know you're tired," says Rumi.
"But come, this is the way."

Maya was my little Rumi.

Okay, I was up, but I felt so sad. I didn't miss the temple in the adult sense; in fact, I felt liberated from the confines of Humanistic Judaism and relieved to be able to explore my own spirituality. I didn't even miss the songs that I'd sung my entire life. No, I missed the temple the way a child longs to move back to her old neighborhood and sleep in her old bedroom or play in her old backyard. I missed the carpet, the chairs, the sound of the big wooden entrance door that squeaked on its hinges and required two hands to push open. I had been pushing that door open since I was seven years old. For me, it was like a castle door. And when I became the rabbi—it felt just like that—like I had been given the keys to the kingdom.

August 1, 2012, Journal Entry:

> *"The temple is my home*
> *womb of my beginning.*
> *My bones are its bones.*
> *My blood, its blood.*
> *How can I detach from the body of my childhood?*
> *Will the machines go off in the ICU?*
> *And the doctors come rushing in?*
> *Will my heart know how to pump*
> *Outside the cavity*
> *Where it has lodged all these years?*

In Hebrew the word *homiyah* means longing. It is used to describe the sound that birds make when they roll back their wings and croon. It's the sound of the bird longing to go home. In the opening verse of Israel's national anthem, *homiyah* is used to describe how the Jewish soul felt during 2,000 years of exile. I knew the feeling well. I longed. I crooned. I missed the temple on a visceral level; it was an overwhelming feeling of, "I just want to go home."

I wasn't a Humanistic Jew anymore. I definitely wasn't a member of the temple. Was I still a rabbi? They couldn't "defrock" me. Could they? Maybe there was a road back. Had I burned the bridge? Did I want to go back?

No. Absolutely not. There was no road, no bridge and no, I didn't want to go back.

I went to see my therapist. She listened intently as I described how scared I was, then tilted her head and asked, "Do you believe that the Universe brought you this far only to drop you on your ass?"

This was a very good question. What *did* I believe? I knew in my gut that I was doing the right thing and that I was being guided by a force. But what was this force? Was it God? It was too soon to name. I lacked the vocabulary. I only knew that it was there. I also knew that though I hurt, something profoundly important and necessary was happening in me. At night when I started to cry, I hushed myself to sleep by whispering over and over again: *Just when the caterpillar thought the world was over, she became a butterfly.*

I called upon the spirit of my grandmother, who lived in me with such profound clarity that even twenty years after her death I could still smell her perfume.

When my grandmother was about my age, her life too changed forever and she found herself alone and scared. Then she took all her anxiety and all her sadness and did something extraordinary: She became *exceedingly brave.*

I had the grandma that every girl needs to become her own heroine. In her quiet way, step by step, my grandmother modeled the journey from being imprisoned by phobias and insecurity to living a joyful and loving life. It took her an entire lifetime and I was the lucky duck who got a front row seat to watch her take the quantum leap to self-love in her final years.

My grandmother's mother died when she was eleven years old. Then her father left and she was sent to live with her older sister. There was often not enough money for rent and they were always moving to avoid being evicted. When my grandmother married my grandfather and they bought a modest home in Detroit, she felt safe for the first time in her life. But there was still so much to overcome! She was afraid of drowning and would not even take a bath. She did not know how to drive or use a checkbook. She depended on my grandfather for almost everything, until, while still in his fifties, he died.

My grandmother had to learn to drive, manage money, raise her youngest daughter and go out into the world by herself. Most of all, she had to find her joy.

When I was ten years old, I taught her how to swim. She laid her head back and floated in my arms. She was so scared but I knew she trusted me, her young granddaughter. She was determined to live the last half of her life differently from the first. She was done being afraid.

That day, the small pool at her apartment complex became as sacred as a baptismal font or a mikvah.

I watched her emancipate herself from all the fears that had drained her over the years. She healed from shame, grew radiant, told jokes (dirty ones, but never to me!) and drove around in a two-door baby blue Chevrolet. She found joy, laughter and, as family matriarch, she showered us with love. Never was I happier, more at peace as a child or teenager than when I was with my Grandma Jeanette. For my master's degree thesis, I interviewed her. She was dying from lymphoma. These are her words:

> *When I was a child there was no one there to say, "I love you," or when I came home from school to ask me, "How was your day?" All my life I felt like I was climbing a tall wall. It was brick, that's how hard it felt. But I just climbed, step by step. Now at the end of my life, I can say to myself, "Jeanette, you did it! You climbed the wall!" It is such a good feeling. I climbed the wall and on the other side I discovered a secret garden. There are roses and peonies. This is my garden. I did it. I made it!*

I had to find a way to be as brave as my grandmother. I wanted to be deserving of my place in the sisterhood of all the brave and loving women who had come before me. I wanted to be able to say to them, "We are kindred spirits. I was brave, too. I walked through the thicket, faced the fire, and found my way little by little, step by step, until one day I too realized: I am growing my own garden."

But how? How do you take all that has been uprooted in your life and make out of it something new and flourishing?

My grandmother tapped into something that was in her, but it was also a force all around her. She tapped into Divine consciousness. I would come to understand this consciousness as the Great Mother, but at the time, I couldn't name it. I could only feel it. My grandmother finally realized that she was lovable just because she was born. She did not have to earn love or defend love. She could never lose love. In essence, she became it.

My grandmother became Love.

Rabbi Seeking Spiritual Home

A month after my resignation, I went to see a lawyer. We met weekly for several months and put together a case for slander. First, we tried to negotiate a severance. After this failed my lawyer advised me: "You need to know that if you decide to sue, you'll be caught up in depositions with them and the case may go on for years." I didn't want to be in a relationship with hatred for years. I didn't think I could take the poison. And there was something more: I couldn't imagine suing Rabbi Wine's temple. I knew what Rabbi Wine would say: "It is beneath you."

I was struggling hour by hour to detox. I had this compulsive track running through my mind. I couldn't get their voices out of my head. I just kept replaying the scenes over and over again on a loop. I wasn't sure where the line was between "their" bad behavior and my own. I knew I didn't deserve the way I was treated but I also knew that I had contributed to the drama. I had fanned the fire. I had argued and fought, too. I had been fighting with people for years. Even if I couldn't imagine how I would have gotten the job otherwise, I was still responsible for my own energy.

"I have lived on the lip
of insanity, wanting to know reasons,
knocking on a door," says Rumi. "It opens.
I've been knocking from the inside."

Should I sue them? No. This time, I had to choose Grace. New Rules: I was going to protect myself. I would not allow myself to be mistreated, nor would I mistreat others. Both were toxic. No more drama, mama. I was going to heal and go forward, not backward. It wasn't worth the money. I felt that I would accumulate karmic debt if I didn't cut the cord now. Visa debt was one thing. Karmic debt was quite another.

It wasn't about the people on the other side of my office door. It was about me. I had to learn to treat myself better, to care for myself and to forgive myself. The other people were just noise. They didn't matter. I had to get right with myself. I had to stop fighting with them and start fighting for myself. I longed for unconditional love, unconditional understanding and deep rest. I longed to be held and rocked. I needed tenderness. I didn't want to be right or prove them wrong. (Well, maybe a little.) But more than anything, I just wanted relief. I had to free myself so that I could live the next chapter of my life, even if I did not know what that would be. Otherwise I would be living in the past, tied to it, cursed and defined by it. My friend told me about the term, "Past Present." It's used to describe the way we live when we cannot let go of the past. If most of our energy is in the past, we do not really have a present. I couldn't let that happen to me.

I decided to take the enormous file from the lawyer's office out to the recycling bin. I thought it belonged in there, not only to save the trees but because the recycling bin had proper symbolic meaning. All the ugliness captured on those pages would be shredded and might possibly become something new. What was written in those files wasn't garbage; it chronicled the most painful period of my life. Still, it needed to be shredded. I heaved the huge binder over the top of the bin and it landed inside with a decisive thud.

Isaac and I decided that we had to sell our house because we could no longer afford the payments. This wasn't altogether a bad thing. I had this incredibly strong urge to leave things behind. I couldn't bear seeing the streets that I'd turned down for so many years on the way to work. I hated living so close to the temple now. I needed a new address to begin my new life. Then I remembered some of my mother's friends who had divorced, moved away and found that their problems moved right along with them.

"Geographical cures don't work," my mother cautioned me.

I weighed this advice against my impulse to sell my house and found that the urge was still overwhelming. *Go. Go,* I heard. We put our house on the market and it sold five days later. I took this as a sign. I was beginning to understand.

When we listen to the Divine whisper, the Universe cooperates. When we resist, the Universe kicks our ass.

I had to learn how to distinguish between ego and intuitive wisdom. When I was listening to my ego, I was suffering. But when I was able to tune into intuitive wisdom, I had a sense that everything would somehow be okay, perhaps even better than I could imagine. It wasn't difficult to discern these two voices once I got a feel for it. My ego talked to me about pain in the past and told me scary stories about my future. My ego was obsessed with scarcity; it wanted me to believe that I would never get another good job or be as whole as I once was. Intuitive wisdom was all about being in the present, and when I listened to this voice I found that I began to look at my situation with more hope, wonder even. My ego told me to sue because I needed money. Intuitive wisdom told me that there would be plenty of money in the future. I used intuitive wisdom to make all the critical first round of decisions, from leaving the temple and discarding the lawsuit to selling my house.

I began tuning inward all the time, deciphering, distinguishing, listening in silence, singing out loud, drumming, howling and experimenting with how to touch a current of loving energy that was both outside and inside of me. Now I waited eagerly for everyone to leave home in the morning so I could unleash myself. I took out the rain stick I'd brought back from Santa Fe and danced rain dances that I made up as I went along. When I grew tired of making it rain in my bedroom, I went outside to be with the trees and feed the birds. I asked for relief from the poisonous apples rolling around in my head. I asked for the courage to move on. *Release me! Heal me! Let me be a great source of abundant Love!* Then, one day, I realized what I was doing. For the first time in my life, I was actually *praying.*

I needed a job. But how was I going to get a job in my state of mind? I had so little confidence and I was in so much internal upheaval. "You'll never find a job like this again" and "Who is going to hire you?" said those goddamn poisonous apples in my head. That's when David called.

David was the director of the premier community funeral chapel in the Detroit area. He was well-respected in the community but I didn't know him very well. I had kept my distance from the "Jewish establishment" because I always felt like an outsider. Add to that the fact that he was a man. I didn't trust men the way I trusted women. I'm close to men in my family but I have always chosen women as friends. Yet when David invited me to lunch, I found myself accepting.

David's timing was impeccable. He didn't know anything that was going on with me, or how deeply I needed to talk with someone like him. We sat down at an outside table.

"How's it going?" he asked casually.

I proceeded to tell him everything, describing the entire catastrophe: the police, my car, the board, my resignation and most of all, how lost I felt. I heard myself talk and talk and talk. I sang like a canary. I was surprised at how much I needed to say and how safe I felt talking to him.

When I had said absolutely everything, he replied, "You need to know one thing. I don't care what the board says. I hear people talk about you all the time and you are not just a rabbi. You are a beloved rabbi."

David began referring funerals to me. There was a niche of families who were not affiliated with a temple and who wanted a service that was "spiritual but not religious." In addition, many families actually liked the idea of working with a female rabbi. Without being asked, David paid me early and put the checks in my mailbox. It was just enough money to get my family by while I figured out what to do with the rest of my life. He became an incredible friend.

Something else happened, too: The community continued to call on me. Many people requested me to conduct services for them, even members of the temple. I was still a rabbi. You could say that funerals gave me my life back.

It is easy to admire people who are at the top of their game. We want what they have: confidence, influence, talent, money. We are always idealizing people who we think have it all. It is far more valuable to befriend each other when we are at our lowest, when we are most vulnerable and even desperate.

When someone comes for you when you are most in need, know this: They are your angel.

I learned that angels come in many different forms, even men in suits from the "establishment." So many barriers were breaking down for me. I was becoming free of long-held assumptions and insecurities that had kept me isolated from really good people.

Before one particular funeral, the caregiver for the person who had died introduced herself to me by saying, "I told her when we met that I was going to be her angel." It was true. The family had already conveyed to me that their mother and caregiver were the best of friends. They went to baseball games, the casino, and when that was no longer possible, sat quietly and held hands.

I believe there are times in our lives when we feel most vulnerable that open us to receive blessings that would not otherwise be available to us. These are the times that invite the angels to come out.

It was in the midst of all this that I found myself searching for a new temple. Our son Lior was turning thirteen in four months. The date for his Bar-Mitzvah had been on the calendar for two years. We still had the Bar-Mitzvah boy and we still had the rabbi, but we didn't have the temple. And we didn't have a lot of time.

I decided to visit a small congregation near our new neighborhood that was described as being warm, progressive and traditional.

Isaac and I went to meet with the rabbi. He greeted us at the front door with open arms. He listened to our situation and generously offered to let me lead Lior's service there. We went inside to look at the sanctuary, and it took my breath away. Not because it was grand – actually, it was quite modest—but because it was filled with beautiful natural light and the trees outside the windows swayed in the breeze behind the arc. It felt organic and sacred. It felt holy, like a space that could hold the breath of God.

The rabbi enthusiastically invited us to get involved and attend services. Isaac didn't say anything. He was along for the Bar-Mitzvah ride but had no intention of getting involved in a temple again. When we got home, we had a family meeting. Lior made it very clear that he was on the same bus as his dad—the Bar-Mitzvah-only bus. I, however, wanted to ride all the buses!

I joined the new temple and told myself that I was going back to Sunday School. I was going to learn what it was as if to include God in my life. I would learn all the prayers, chant them, memorize them and experience their meaning. I would learn the traditional order to the Shabbat service, Bar Mitzvah service, and every other service. I sat in the congregation with a pen and a notebook, numbering and mapping the new theater in front of me: the rabbi stands, the Torah is opened, the people bow, the crown on the Torah is jingled. These are all things that a child growing up in a congregation learns intuitively by repetition. I wanted to be as authentic as that child. I wanted to be like a native and merge seamlessly into the prayer body of Israel.

While the rest of my family was home watching Netflix, I combed the internet for videos of any and all Shabbat services. I checked out websites for every congregation that appealed to me and listened to their cantors. It was a new world for me and I found it delicious. The prayers came easily in large part because I was already fluent in Hebrew. Before long I was sailing along in my new spiritual home.

One day the rabbi at the new temple asked me if I would be interested in leading the services. *He trusted me to do that? I could be back on the bima as a rabbi?* It seemed actually unbelievable.

And the blessings kept coming. An older woman in the community, who considered herself both a Jew and a Buddhist, invited me to her home. I first met her after her husband died and had been visiting with her ever since. At ninety-four years old, she sat holding a meditation puck with her legs elevated and talked to me about Kundalini yoga, the power of breath and the life force energy of the Universe.

"Rabbi Kolton," she said, "I'm going to help you, but there are terms for accepting this money. When you are able, you have to find a worthy young woman and help her along her way, too."

That sounded perfect. Sign me up!

The money was directed to fund my work at the new temple. I would be the scholar in residence for eighteen months. I now had a nice window of time before I had to worry about finding a job and could immerse myself in the liturgy of Judaism and all the holidays and services at the new synagogue. I felt happy and expectant. I had butterflies in my stomach.

For the next year and a half, I conducted services, taught classes and developed a curriculum I called "Soulful Living." The classes were very special. Each time we met, I led a group as small as twenty or as large as a hundred in exploring one of the essential Jewish prayers.

I also asked the class to explore the Hebrew letters as holy transportation vehicles. The Hebrew letters bound the Jews together after they were scattered to the four corners of the Earth. The temple in Jerusalem could be destroyed by ancient Rome and the Jewish people exiled from their land, but the letters were untouchable. They were light as air, indestructible, and they didn't require a temple or even a Torah. In Krakow, Casablanca, and Barcelona, the Jews prayed in Hebrew. A Jew spoke Chinese, Hungarian, Arabic, or Russian outside of the synagogue, but spoke Hebrew inside. To this day, a Jew can walk into a synagogue anywhere in the world on Shabbat and join in prayer.

I fell in love with Hebrew when I was sixteen on a youth trip to Israel. I also fell in love with Israel and young Israeli men in uniform (more on that later). For me, learning Hebrew felt more like remembering a language that I used to know. I loved the feel of the guttural sounds in the back of my throat and how assertive I became when I spoke it in the streets of Jerusalem. Hebrew pumped through me like oxygen. I ran to catch the bus in Hebrew calling out "Rak rega!" ("Wait for me!") I shopped in the open-air market in Hebrew, bargaining down a kilo of cucumbers by challenging the vendor, "Yoter-mi-diey!" ("Too much!") I breathed in the consonants and breathed out the vowels like vital gases needed by my blood.

Sometimes, when I was teaching the prayers to the class, I worried that I was getting overly excited. I surveyed the faces of the students. Did they think I was crazy, too emotional, or as one past critic complained, "Too Kumbaya?" No. They looked very comfortable. Actually, they looked excited, too. I felt like an elephant finally getting to roll in some really cool mud.

Skiing into the Spiritual Crevasse of Patriarchy

It seemed like the trek uphill was finally over. I can't tell you how good that felt! Instead of a mountain climber, I now felt like a pro skier slaloming downhill with the wind at my back, feeling the *swoosh* and *whoosh* of a great run. Look at all the effort I had expended and how I'd sweated out the unknown! Ha! It was all behind me now. I had found a new place to belong. That's what I was feeling when I skied right down into the spiritual crevasse.

Everything stopped. Everything went silent. Everything froze.

One minute I was standing in the pew at the new temple *davening (*praying) and the next it was as if the ground had caved in beneath me.

All I could hear down there in the crevasse was the echo of, "He." "He" is the Ruler. "He" is Shepherd. "He" is the Father, Host, Lord and King. The modern prayer book included a few gender-neutral translations, but they were "additions." And then there was the unavoidable fact that the men who wrote the prayers never

41

intended for me to say them. In fact, if they were alive and walked into the temple where I was praying, they wouldn't sit next to me. They would expect me to give them my seat. They might even spit on me. *Are their words* my *words? Is this how I talk to God? Do these prayers even belong to me?* Suddenly I felt so illegitimate, as if I was in the wrong family.

For millennia, Jewish men shut Jewish women out from the world of prayer, relegating them to sit behind a veiled partition or watch the service from a balcony. Women were not taught to read and write Hebrew. In Judaism, a minimum number of ten people is required for public worship. This quorum is called a Minyan. Historically, women were never counted in the Minyan. The role of women was to enable men to study the Torah so men could grow close to God. In the Talmud, the rabbinic scholars wrote, "These are the tasks that a wife must carry out for her husband: She must grind corn, bake, wash, cook, suckle her child, make her husband's bed and knit with wool." The most revered rabbis warned the men, "Don't go near a woman."

In Orthodox Judaism, a woman is considered too spiritually impure to touch the Torah. Why? Because she might be bloody. Even in menopause. Orthodox Jews believe that menstrual blood is a source of ritual impurity so a man must never be in contact with it. After a woman menstruates, she must wait seven days, go to the *mikvah* (the ritual bath) and immerse herself completely three times. Then and only then may her husband touch her. These laws are recorded in the Talmud in a book called *Nidah*, meaning, "the state of purity." If a woman gives birth to a girl, her husband must wait fourteen days before he can touch her. She's extra dirty then. He can't even hold her hand.

One day when my son was very young he looked up at me in the kitchen and declared, "Dad is a *much* better cook than you. A man's place is in the kitchen. Women should be rabbis. Men should be cooks."

Lior was on to something. There was no turning back time to make me a corn-grinding, wool- knitting woman. All the origami in the world could not fold me back into patriarchy's daughter.

During my nearly two decades of being a rabbi, I unabashedly challenged the Jewish establishment about the subordinate role of women. I wrote my doctoral dissertation on it! But since I had never considered God to be real, my activism was political, not spiritual. I was comfortable being an advocate for Jewish women in leadership, but at the time, it honestly didn't matter to me if God was described as a man or a tomato. Now, God was vital for me. I wasn't just a feminist. I was a Jewish woman coming into her spiritual power and yearning to discover God. Rita M Gross writes in *On Being a Jewish Feminist*, "One begins to sense that God, as well as women, has been imprisoned in patriarchal imagery." I couldn't help but agree with her. There was an absence—a missing piece, or parts of a piece missing—and thus there was no whole.

Feminine spirituality so often begins in the void; we are sitting there in the pews of our temples or churches and we can't help but long for something more, even though we don't necessarily know what that something is.

This longing is the call of the Feminine Divine. It's as if She is signaling to us, "Hey! Over Here! I'm here! Can you see me?" We especially long for Her as we outgrow former structures, former roles, former ways of living in the world. In that painful ache of, "There must be more for me," She is present.

We sense the emptiness through the absence of fullness. A full experience of the Divine must fully include the feminine. If the language of the service is explicit in which the names for God are called out, they must also include Her name—not as an addition or a footnote, but equally and reverently. Otherwise, as women, we feel like the teacher just took attendance and didn't call our name.

Judith Plaskow, a leader in Jewish feminism, writes it this way:

> The need for a feminist Judaism begins with hearing silence. It begins with noting the absence of women's history and experience as shaping forces of the Jewish tradition. Women

have lived Jewish history, carried its burdens, but women's perceptions and questions have not given form to scripture, shaped the direction of Jewish law, or found expression in liturgy.

Sitting there in the pew, I fight the urge to raise my hand and ask the rabbi, *"Excuse me if I've been living in a bubble all my life, but has God always been a man? I know, I know. It's just a metaphor. But can't God be a woman?* How can I ever believe in God unless I trust God to believe in me...*all of me?"*

The congregation rises and the Torah is removed from the arc, the silver crown jingles as the scroll is undressed and unwrapped. This is the holiest moment. It is the time when the words of the scroll will be exposed to air. Every Torah is handwritten by a scribe who must make it painstakingly perfect. No letter can be crossed out or redone. That is why the pages are stitched together in small sections. If the scribe makes a mistake, he only has to start again from the beginning of the section. Otherwise, he would have to start from the beginning of the scroll! The Torah is the first five books of the Hebrew Bible and every word has to be exactly as it was first written down some 2,500 years ago.

I tried. Baby, how I tried! I showed up like a rabbi ready for the Revival. I wanted it so badly. I wanted to feel what I knew was possible to feel even though I had hardly ever felt it in my life. It's as if I remembered the feeling but forgot the specs on when or where or how. I knew there was a path back to God, a way of feeling at One with the Divine. *I knew it.* Like it is when you wake up from a dream and you know exactly what you dreamed until you actually begin to think about it. Once you run the metaphors and the magic through the mind, the dream evaporates. *If I could remember how to be a butterfly, I could fly out of here, out of the crevasse,* I thought. But by now my hands and feet were beginning to freeze. I knew there was no way I'd ever fly out of that crevasse unless I was willing to become something else. I had to come to understand who I was in a different way. I had to realize how to nourish myself with the Divine nectar that I needed so that I could build the strength to do what I was always meant to do: Soar.

Metamorphosis begins in your cells, not in your mind. It is an uncomfortable, unstoppable force.

You cannot stop the caterpillar in you from becoming a butterfly.

Once you outgrow your former nature, you must find a way to become something new. Otherwise you'll die. Thelma says it best when she tells Louise, "...you know, something's like crossed over in me and I can't go back. I mean, I just couldn't live."

Like Thelma, I couldn't go back. I could not fit myself into a patriarchal structure. I would always be a Jew and be proud to be a Jew. But something crossed over in me. Some bridges are meant to be saved and crossed back over, but others are meant to be burned.

I was burning all the bridges that constricted my spirit. Unabashedly, bonfire style, I could not help but yearn to burn everything that restricted my true nature, all the need for approval from Rabbi Wine, the board, Patriarchy, the pain in my childhood, and all the voices steamrolling through my head. I had to find my own way of feeling right in the world.

October 2012, Journal Entry:

I grow kindred with all animals who shed and molt

The snake, lizard, crayfish and butterfly

I like that I am cousin to this creepy creature family

Where metamorphosis is normal and necessary.

I want to wear my skin with the timing and grace of a hermit crab

Who knows exactly when she has outgrown her home

And exactly how to grow a new one.

It was a big hard time, the kind you look back on and think to yourself, "Thank God *that* is over!" But it was a very important time as well. I ached and swelled and wiggled with all my might to release myself from every tight place I had ever been in. I was becoming right with my inner nature. I was growing my wings. I could feel it everywhere.

"Our mess isn't ugly or unmanageable. It isn't something that needs to be slicked down, bent into shape, or shoved into a dark closet. It is the very source of our beauty and power, our passion and strength."
~Kelly McNelis

It was time to finally do the deepest healing that I needed to do. It was time to address a core sadness and shame that I had carried my entire life. It was time to take off my f*ing fig leaf.

Spiritual Exercise

What Is Your Butterfly Story?

1. What is your butterfly story?

2. Who is your Grandma Jeanette?

3. Can you think of a time in your life when you were "down on your knees"? Who came for you? Who are your human angels?

4. Divide a piece of paper in three. In the first third, draw a picture of the God you grew up with. In the second, draw a picture of God for you today. In the third, draw a picture of what God can be for you. What do you notice?

5. What would you do if you knew with 100% certainty that you would not fail?

Journaling Space

_____

_____

_____

_____

_____

_____

_____

_____

_____

_____

_____

_____

_____

_____

_____

_____

_____

_____

_____

_____

_____

_____

_____

_____

_____

The Third Day

The F*ing Fig Leaf

Expulsion from the Garden of Eden, 1425, Masaccio, *Cacciata*

"Then the eyes of both of them were opened, and they realized they were naked; so they sewed fig leaves together and made coverings for themselves."
~Genesis 3:7

In the Beginning... We Were Shamed

*M*y mother has a saying about dating: "It's all there in the beginning." Everything undesirable about the person sitting across from us at the table—the sides of him that we will later claim he *never showed us*—are right there next to the saltshaker. If he hasn't worked or talked to his mother in a year, or says he only smokes once in a while—it's there. If he is still married but *going* to get divorced or needs you to pay for dinner *just this one time*—you can face it or deny it—but it's all there, *in the beginning.*

It's all there for us too, *in the beginning.* In Genesis, the first story about a woman is the same excruciating story that most women will live out all the days of their lives: "Then the eyes of both of them were opened and they realized they were naked; so, they sewed fig leaves together and made themselves coverings." (Genesis 3:7)

The first emotion Eve felt after she was banished from Eden was shame. In fact, Eve only realized that she was naked because she felt ashamed of her body. Shame drove her to put on a fig leaf. That's how God knew she had eaten the apple. He saw her with a fig leaf on.

In the beginning, we were taught to hate our bodies.

"The difference between shame and guilt," writes Brené Brown, "is the difference between 'I am bad', and 'I did something bad.'" Eve didn't just feel guilty. She felt ashamed. She wanted to disappear. Can you imagine what it must have felt like for her, suddenly thrust under the spotlight of the most powerful being comprehensible. And he was enraged! The pain must have been excruciating. We are only told that she covered herself up. The Bible never tells us anything about what it was like to actually be Eve.

This is how I imagine what it was like to actually be Eve:

"What have you done?" God thunders at Eve.

Startled, she looks up from the thicket—caught in the act of desperately grabbing a fig leaf.

"What have you done?" He thunders again, louder than any sound she has ever heard. So loud that it hurts! It hurts!

Eve wants to tell God that she thought eating the apple was the right thing to do, that she was just following her intuition, that she and Adam needed to learn how to trust themselves—that she would still be good and pure and... But she is absolutely sure that until she covers her body she will be unable to speak. The most powerful being is looking at her and she is naked. She knows that she must have done something very bad but does not know what it is. She wants to apologize, explain—protest! But she cannot speak. Her throat is completely closed. She is gagging inside. All she can do is put on a fig leaf.

Eve has just lost everything—her entire world has been destroyed and her primary preoccupation is to find a fig leaf so she can cover up her vagina.

The loss of Paradise first shows up as a woman's rejection of her own body. Sadly, this is not just true for Eve, but for every woman born after her. It's unbelievable, really.

51

What is a F*ing Fig Leaf?

Yeah, it's not just a fig leaf, it's a *f*ing* fig leaf. That's how awful, powerful, burdensome, devastating and absurd it is, and we all wear one. Our fig leaves are made up of the fibers of our shame and woven into our psyches stitch by stitch, not because we actually did anything wrong, but because we were born female. Our fig leaves are the voices inside us and around us that say, "Don't you dare!" or "You'll never…" or "It's your fault…" A woman's fig leaf might be how she feels—fat, disgusting, ugly, too tall, too short, too loud, too brown, or too black. A woman might wear her fig leaf in the way she just cannot bring herself to vote for a female president.

In my work as a psychologist, I have a client who is healing her body image. In our session, I talk to her about the whole fig leaf idea. "When I get up in the morning," she says, "I reach to put on my fig leaf before I reach for my glasses."

Our fig leaves grow on us as we grow old, too. Consider how painful it is for an aging woman to accept herself and be acceptable to society. Men get to grow old gracefully, but we nip, tuck, make it up, and attempt to squeeze it all in. For a woman, aging is painful. For a woman, aging is loss.

Our fig leaves are the ways that our joy, radiance and power are shut down or go unexpressed, and it happens all day long from middle school to the corporate world; in the city and in the suburbs. Why? Because deep inside the psyche of women and men, there is a powerful, primal force at work which consciously or unconsciously keeps a woman from ever daring to do the most dreadfully disruptive and intimately awful of all things: take off her f*ing fig leaf.

Rather than do that, we are taught how to be a "good girl," a helpful, nice girl. The more we help, the nicer we appear, the more we are rewarded. Consider that in the Bible, Eve was created because Adam was lonely. God created Eve from Adam's rib to make Adam feel better. Biblically speaking, helping Adam to feel better was Eve's entire reason for existence. Without him, she evaporates.

"This may be the fundamental problem with caring a lot about what others think: It can put you on the established path—the my-isn't-that-impressive path—and keep you there for a long time. Maybe it stops you from swerving, from ever even considering a swerve, because what you risk losing in terms of other people's high regard can feel too costly."
~Michelle Obama

Amazingly... Miraculously... Awesomely... One day, Eve decided to swerve. I wonder, *What made her do it?* What change had to occur in Eve so that she finally understood that she was not born solely to help Adam? She might love Adam with all her soul. She might choose to be with Adam and devote herself to him. But Eve was not created to make Adam's life easier.

Eve was born to be Eve.

The moment that Eve began to think about doing something on her own (i.e. picking that apple), she became her own person. She claimed her own identity, her own voice and her dignity.

The moment that Eve's hand touched the forbidden fruit is the most sacred moment in all the Bible.

When Eve picked the apple, she connected to her own Divinity. *And what could be seen as more dangerous than a woman connected to the truth of who she really is?* What would happen if more women acted like Eve? Imagine the consequences of an entire generation of women who insisted on being their own people!

No one knows exactly how old the myth of Eve is. But we do know that the Hebrew Bible (the Old Testament) was canonized about 2,000 years ago. This means that this story was selected to be included in the Bible by those who held religious power at the time. There must have been hundreds of myths about the creation of women, so why was this particular version chosen above the others? Because it contained the perfect poison, concocted of just the right ingredient to shut down feminine power, truth and light. That ingredient is shame. Well, we have to hand it to them—it was ingenious, and much more efficient than pinning a scarlet letter on every female born for the next 2,000 years. Instead, they just hung this toxic story around our necks, a poisonous mythology that renewed itself in every generation. And even if you stopped telling us the story, you could bet on one thing: We would tell it to ourselves.

That, *my dear sister,* is the f*ing fig leaf.

How Do You Wear Yours?

I'm six years old and standing in my bedroom in front of the double door blue armoire. I am getting myself dressed. I open the doors and choose the red overalls, not because I like them or because they are comfortable; I choose them because *they don't make me look fat.* I remember picking them out from underneath a pile of clothing with only that thought in my mind. I remember stepping into them, pulling them up and buckling them. I remember what kind of red they were, a rusty red and the kind of fabric they were made of, a soft, light cotton. I remember the buckles and the pockets.

I do not have any recollection of any other clothing I wore as a child, other than what I've seen in photos. But I remember those overalls because they were the first piece of clothing I ever put on not to wear *on* my body but *to cover it up.* They marked my fall from Grace. They marked a change in consciousness from *just being in my body* to judging my body. How? How did it happen? Somehow,

I got the message that I was bigger than other girls, that I would look better (i.e. smaller) if I dressed a certain way. I have no idea if someone said something to me or if I heard someone say something to someone else. Was it because my mother was skinny and I was so obviously not? Or a thousand other social cues buzzing around on a typical American day like mosquitos looking for someone to bite?

On that particular day, at that particular time, something died in me. I stopped being "just me." I stopped choosing what I like to wear, what I thought was soft or beautiful to my eyes, and began wearing what would make me look a certain way. I stopped dressing for myself and I began dressing for someone else. I stopped feeling good in my skin and I began feeling ashamed of my body. I traded in my internal knowing for external approval. All this when I was still young enough to believe that my stuffed animals were real and desperately needed me to adopt them from the corner drugstore. All this when I still sucked my thumb to fall asleep at night. And the thing is, my story is not unusual. I bet you have one that is very similar. I bet you know exactly the day and time and where you were standing in the room when you began to reject yourself too.

*How old were you when you first put on your F*ing Fig Leaf?*

Another memory:

I am eight years old and standing on the gymnastic vault. I am the youngest gymnast on the team. Today I'm doing a somersault dismount and Coach Angie is spotting me when she looks up and asks, "When are you going to lose weight?"

I'm dumbfounded. Completely speechless. I cannot speak. All I can do is look around the warehouse gym at the tiny girls in leotards. They are poised and pointed and flying through the air like weightless birds. Suddenly I feel about as weightless as an elephant. I want to disappear, but I'm too big. If shame could be measured and quantified, in an instant a four-hundred-pound burden attached itself to my energy field.

It was a spiritual attack on my birthright—the birthright of every woman—to appreciate her body as a marvelous system of energy in motion, her portion of Divine stardust. It was the moment when I felt banished from Eden.

Body-shaming is a modern-day witch hunt. In a patriarchal society, it is the way female power is drained.

As long as we hate ourselves, and pass that hate down to future generations, we will never have the energy to challenge the structures of power and the mythology around us. It's like asking yourself to go jogging when you have the stomach flu. Not possible. When you have the stomach flu all you have energy to do is hug the toilet. The stomach flu is a total distraction. *Shame is like the stomach flu. It keeps you functioning on such a low level that you can barely cope with the pain of being you; as long as it's in your system you'll never have what you need to get up from the bathroom floor, look around and demand a little more for yourself.*

Today, at forty-nine years old, I realize that the only thing indecent about my body is how I treat it. I have spent thousands of days sick with the "stomach flu," feeling guilty and ashamed of myself. There has not been a single morning when I have not judged myself, evaluated myself, compared myself and been mean to myself. Even on days when I escape into the miracle of feeling pretty for a brief, blessed moment, there's always the thought—"Don't gain it back!"—lurking just behind the mirror. I am never really free.

A few years ago, I dreamt that I was diagnosed with a deadly form of cancer. In the dream, I knew with absolute certainty that I was going to die soon. But I wasn't worried about that. Instead, I was absolutely consumed with remorse and guilt over dying before I lost weight. I'd squandered my last chance to live in a thin body. *There's no more time. You blew it,* I thought to myself in the dream as I walked down a flight of stairs to tell my family that I was going to die.

I do not know of any woman who likes, let alone loves, the way she looks. There are only the women who suffer more and those who suffer less. I know women who are learning how to accept themselves as they grow older, but I do not know anyone who does not have to work at it—hard.

I believe the poison first gets into our system from an external bite. We are "shamed." It comes from outside of us. Someone shames us and we get the message that we are disgraceful—lacking grace and disgusting. Since we are social animals, this is absolutely terrifying.

But this is long-acting poison. It continues to work on an internal level. We feed it to ourselves maybe a thousand times a day by what we say to ourselves inside our own heads. These messages that we send to ourselves are the deadliest.

You know those mattress commercials, the ones in which they tell you how many years you'll spend in bed during your lifetime because they want you to invest in an uber-expensive, fully adjustable memory foam sleep number you-won't-hear-your-husband-snoring-all-night–or-feel-the-ache-in-your-middle-aged-almost-ar-thritic-left-hip mattress? How many thousands and thousands of hours have I spent laying in a bed of deprecating, soul-slaying messages, from me to me, about my body? How many thousands and thousands of hours have I spent obsessing about what I weigh and what I should weigh? More than age, numbers on the scale define my life. In college, I weighed 172. In high school, I weighed 169. In junior high, I weighed 127. As I write these words, I weigh 181. (Did I tell you I'm five feet tall and think I should weigh less than 135?) The way people refer to eras like, "Back in the 50s," is how I reference my weight. In the Bible, a generation is forty years. I've been around since the 70s, which means I have been at war with my flesh for an entire generation.

Clearly, it's time for a new mattress.

Middle School and the Day I Forgot to Put My Bra On

Sometime in seventh grade, I began to reject my body on a conscious level. I remember feeling horrified one morning after being picked up for school by the neighborhood carpool. Just as we pulled into the school parking lot, I realized I had forgotten to put on my bra. I was wearing a heavy sweatshirt and on any other day I might have managed, but not this day: *Oh God,* I thought, *today I have Gym.*

By seventh grade, I had my Grandma Vi's boobs. They were significant. Years before, I remember visiting my grandparents in Florida and using their bathroom. Over the back of the door, there was an enormous contraption. I just stood there and stared at it, trying to work out what it was and why it was hanging on the door. At some point, it hit me that it was my grandmother's bra. *Holy shit,* I thought, *you've got to be kidding me!* That thing was huge. I mean *horse harness* huge. I couldn't believe a person actually had to wear that. A few years later something happened—I became my Grandma Vi.

The day I forgot my bra, I didn't call home and I certainly didn't tell the gym teacher. I didn't even tell a friend over a giggle because it wasn't funny. I just sucked it up in silence. For the next thirty-five years I would feel like that braless teenager, sucking it up while I lugged myself through life, painfully uncomfortable in my own skin, with sporadic, brief, moments of relief.

Seventh grade was also the year I joined Weight Watchers for the first time. (I believe that Weight Watchers was then, and still is, the best program out there.) At the weigh-in, the nice lady in hot pink lipstick handed me my weigh-in card. It read 127 ½. At four-foot-eleven, I needed to lose about fifteen pounds. Two months went by. I returned to the nice lady in hot pink lipstick, stepped on and off the scale and she handed me back my weigh-in card. It read 139 ½. I had gained twelve pounds. My hunger was out of control. At thirteen, I didn't understand the difference between true hunger and trying to fill the deep hole I felt in my gut. I didn't understand that I was really hungry to feel safe, comfortable and relaxed in the world. In *Women Food and God*, Geneen Roth writes:

> We don't want to *eat* hot fudge sundaes as much as we want

our lives to *be* hot fudge sundaes. We want to come home to ourselves. We want to know wonder and delight and passion and instead we've given up on ourselves. If we've vacated our longings, if we've left possibility behind, we will feel an emptiness we can't name. We will feel as if something is missing because something is missing—the connection to the source of all sweetness, all love, all power, all peace, all joy, all stillness.

Looking back, I realize how I used food to cope with the pain I felt in my home. Our house was a beautiful, large modern new build in an upscale neighborhood, but none of us wanted to live there. My mother wanted to get divorced. My father wanted my mother to love him, but his anger made him unlovable. My brother wanted my father to approve of him and I wanted everyone to stop fighting and live in peace. So I "adopted" hundreds of stuffed animals from the dollar store and made them my family. And I ate to comfort myself.

On my sixteenth birthday, Rabbi Wine asked me to stay after Hebrew class.

"Come into my office," he gestured warmly, "I want to talk with you."

Oh God, I thought. *What did I do wrong?*

It was a big deal to go into Rabbi Wine's office. For Humanistic Jews, it was the equivalent of the Oval Office, and you don't just go into the Oval Office. You have to be summoned.

It was a true 1980's style office. Inside there was a way cool, large macramé art piece with brown beads and frayed ends hanging down one wall and an enormous, mostly black painting on another. There were several macramé toss pillows on the sleek, low couch and two expensive matching club chairs. Throw in a chrome swivel chair and wall-to-wall carpeting and, baby, you've got style. If anyone had told me that eighteen years later this inner sanctum would become mine, I would have said there was a better chance of me having an office on the moon.

As Rabbi Wine opened his office door, I saw my mom inside

with a birthday cake. They both sang an off-key but enthusiastic "Happy Birthday to Tammy." I couldn't believe it! Then my mother handed me a card that read, "Happy 16ᵗʰ Birthday to my darling daughter. For your present I am giving you a trip to Israel."

Israeli poet Yehuda Amichai wrote, "The air over Jerusalem is saturated with prayers and dreams /like the air over cities with heavy industry/ It's hard to breathe."

I spent that summer in Israel where, indeed, the air was different, the people were different and—to my surprise and de-light— the concept of beauty was different.

In America, I was an overweight teenager. But in Israel, I was *hot*. By Middle Eastern standards, I wasn't fat, I was "full," and a real blond-haired, blue-eyed head-turner. It was as if I was finally free of a burden I had carried all my life. I literally felt lighter and more alive than ever before. For the first time in I couldn't remember when, I didn't feel at war with my body. For the first time ever, I felt beautiful. Surrounded by eighteen-year-old sun-drenched Israeli soldiers sporting green fatigues and M-16s, I was getting whiplash as well. That summer I hiked—and kissed—my way from the Upper Galilee down to the Judean Desert.

A few years later, I met Isaac from just outside Tel Aviv. We've been married for twenty-three years now. Isaac, thank God, likes "full" women.

How Do We Heal?

So, how do you begin the process of unlearning your shame? Though it's a daunting task, it is within your grasp, using these very effective strategies.

Strategy #1: Spread Your Bravery (The #MeToo Strategy)

In 2006, Tarana Burke made a decision: *She was going to talk about it.* She was going to talk about being a survivor of sexual abuse and encourage other women to talk about it too. She would name names, provide all the gruesome details and stop protecting the identity of anyone who had harmed her.

She had no way of knowing that several years later a famous actress would also come forward with her story, followed by millions of other courageous women, giving birth to the #MeToo movement. At the time, Tarana knew only this: When you speak about your shame and pain, the story no longer owns you. Once you break the code of silence with your abuser, you become powerful.

"You put it out into the world," Tarana says, "It came out your lips. You're still alive. You made it. It's out there and you lived."

All systems of power seek to preserve themselves. This is done by systematically silencing anyone with a dissenting opinion. History is littered with examples of the lengths that authoritarian systems will go to in order to silence people. The circumstances vary from era to era, but the threat is always the same: If you say anything against us, you'll die. The threat of death can be physical, social and/or psychological, but the motive behind it is always the same: To keep the dirt swept under the rug.

But something extraordinary is happening all around us that the establishment did not count on! *We are talking to each other!*

Consider how over the past three decades, the bravest of brave have come forward all over the world to out priests for what is referred to as "sexual abuse" but is more accurately described as the rape of children. We feel the tremendous resistance from the hierarchy of the Catholic Church to acknowledge this abuse and take action. But if the Church won't do anything to protect the children-anything real—the rest of us will, and we will do this by continuing to talk about it. We will never stop. The more we talk, the more we organize and unite, the more powerful we become, because what we are learning is this:

Bravery, like shame, is contagious.

Here, in Michigan, more than two hundred world-class gymnasts recently came forward to talk about the unspeakable abuse they endured at the hands of a predatory doctor. They stood shoulder to shoulder. They lent each other courage. They wept in each other's arms until one by one they broke through the silence, often at nearly unendurable cost. This achievement—this tidal wave of bravery—was a golden contribution to the collective soul of women and anyone who was ever afraid to tell their story.

"We want the world to understand the systems that we are living in that allowed this to happen," explains Tarana Burke.

In 2017, *Time* magazine named the women and men of the #MeToo movement and all "silence-breakers" as their People of The Year.

Indeed, we are living in a most extraordinary time! We see evidence of this everywhere, in the incredible movements springing up to uplift, encourage and honor the power of "saying it out loud." Women and men are joining forces to break through all the shame and silence that perpetrators depend on to commit their crimes. Their secrets just aren't safe anymore, and neither is the paradigm from which they operate.

Questions to Consider:

- *What is your brave story to tell?*

- *Whose bravery do you want to "catch?" Remember, bravery is contagious!*

Strategy #2: Spiritual Disobedience

On October 9, 2012, a masked gunman boarded a school bus in Pakistan. "Which one is Malala?" he demanded.

The gunman was after fifteen-year-old Malala Yousafzai, who had been speaking out against the Taliban-imposed ban on schooling for girls. Using a pen name, Malala blogged for the BBC, writing, "How dare the Taliban take away my basic right to education!"

Four years earlier, in 2008, the Taliban had seized Malala's village and forbid her to attend the egalitarian school that her father founded. In addition to education, the Taliban also banned music and television. Their goal: the total elimination of female participation in social and political life. Malala disagreed.

"The extremists were, and they are, afraid of books and pens," she said. "The power of education frightens them. They are afraid of women... Let us pick up our books and pens. They are our most powerful weapons."

The masked gunman looked around the bus of terrified children and again demanded, "Which one of you is Malala?"

Malala's friends turned to her—an innocent, knee-jerk reaction— and in doing so inadvertently gave her up. The gunman shot her on the left side of the head and left her for dead. He thought she would be silenced. But she was not silenced. Not even close.

Just a year later, Malala stood before the United Nations. "The terrorists thought that they would change our aims and stop our ambitions," she said, "but nothing changed in my life except this: weakness, fear and hopelessness died. Strength, power and courage were born."

In December 2014, Malala received the Nobel Peace Prize. At seventeen years old, she was the youngest person ever to become a Nobel Laureate.

How did she do it? How did she overcome all the intimidation and sheer terror to maintain her truth? "I am one of those sixty-six million girls," she said, "There is a moment when you have to choose whether to be silent or to stand up."

Malala was practicing spiritual disobedience.

Spiritual Disobedience is the art of defending female light.

There was a stunning, radiant light moving through Malala, like the brightest rays of sun. It was the kind of light that radiates from the North Star; the kind of light that guides you to be exceedingly brave and unabashedly daring. Harriet Tubman used that light, literally, to lead slaves to freedom. No one could stop the light that shone from the North Star and no one could stop Harriet Tubman.

"You'll be free or die," she wrote in her diary.

Malala's father explained how he raised Malala to be strong, independent and so very spectacular:

> In Pakistan, the birth of a girl follows a very common pattern: When the girl is born she is not welcomed, neither by father nor by mother... People ask me what is special about my mentorship that made Malala so bold and courageous, vocal and poised. I tell them, "Don't ask me what I did. Ask me what I did not do. I did not clip her wings." (TED2014; Ziauddin Yousafzai)

Of course, there are always consequences for being a disruptive woman. Though not all will face those as extreme as Malala, every woman who insists on following her own truth, on being the agent of her own life, will have to face rejection, ridicule and sometimes much worse. Monica Sjöö and Barbara Mor remind us:

> During the five hundred years of Inquisition, representing the triumph of Christian imperialism over Pagan Europe, a woman could either become a totally subservient wife—beaten and bullied by her husband, her eyes to the ground as the priests and preachers condemned and blamed her sex for all things—or she could stand straight, proud in her own woman-wisdom, and be burnt as a witch.

I remember the exact words of one of the men at the showdown board meeting at which I resigned my pulpit. Furious at something I said, he screamed, "You are an outrageous woman!" Not an "outrageous person" or an "outrageous rabbi," but an "outrageous woman." I was stunned. Here I was, a rabbi at a temple so liberal it was literally falling off the edge of the Jewish world, yet one of its most respected members, with his point of reference, plunged me into the mindset of the Inquisition. An "outrageous woman" was disobedient, incorrigible and powerful; thus, she had to be silenced. If that meeting had taken place five hundred years ago, he would have burnt me at the stake. I'm absolutely sure of it.

Questions to Consider:

- *What cause is most important to you at this time in your life?*

- *Recall the statement of Malala's father: "I did not clip her wings." Who supported or supports you in your journey to fly? Who are you committed to supporting?*

Strategy #3: Celebrate Your Inner Lilith

There is a story in Jewish folklore about a woman who refused to be Adam's "helpmate." Have you heard of her? Her name is Lilith and she is absolutely incorrigible.

Lilith's legend and power grew, especially during the Middle Ages, but she predates that time period by thousands of years. Her name comes from the Hebrew word *lilah*, meaning night. Artists imagine her as a beautiful naked woman with wings and bird feet. She has been referred to as a night owl and a screech owl who nests and lays eggs. And she is out for no good.

Lilith is the shadow of Eve.

We learn about her in The Alphabet of Ben Sira, a collection of stories from the Bible and Talmud dating back to the 8th to 10th centuries CE. In these stories, Lilith comes to life as the unruly wife of Adam who will not play the role of the "little woman," even in the face of dire consequences. Here is her story from The Alphabet of Ben Sira:

> After God created Adam, who was alone, He said, 'It is not good for man to be alone.' He then created a woman for Adam, from the earth, as He had created Adam himself, and called her Lilith. Adam and Lilith immediately began to fight. She said, 'I will not lie below,' and he said, 'I will not lie beneath you, but only on top. For you are fit only to be in the bottom position, while I am to be the superior one.' Lilith responded, 'We are equal to each other inasmuch as we were both created from the earth.' But they would not listen to one another. Since Lilith saw [how it was], she pronounced the Ineffable Name and flew away into the air.
>
> Adam stood in prayer before his Creator: 'Sovereign of the Universe!' he said, 'The woman you gave me has run away.' At once, the Holy One, blessed be He, sent these three angels Senoy, Sansenoy, and Semangelof, to bring her back.
>
> Said the Holy One to Adam, 'If she agrees to come back, what is made is good. If not, she must permit one hundred of her children to die every day.' The angels left God and

pursued Lilith, whom they overtook in the midst of the sea, in the mighty waters wherein the Egyptians were destined to drown. They told her God's orders, but she refused to return.

Because there is no place for a strong, disobedient, self-advocating woman, especially in the society of her day, the only thing to do with a woman like Lilith was to make her into a demon. The death of infants and children is effectively pinned on Lilith; if only she would agree to go home to Adam and submit, the world would be back in balance! But she won't. Ever.

In the late seventies, Jewish feminists claimed Lilith as a sister. Susan Weidman Schneider founded a magazine named *Lilith*, "…in order to foster discussion of Jewish women's issues and put them on the agenda of the Jewish community, with a view to giving women-who are more than fifty percent of the world's Jews—greater choice in Jewish life." Lilith became a great symbol of Jewish feminist activism. Jewish feminists saw her, not as a demon who flies through the night snatching children, but as a role model and a way-shower for how to live a life beyond submission. In a form of creative Jewish writing called Midrash, Jewish women spun great tales about her and embraced her as their heroine. Here are two of my favorites:

Lilith by Enid Dame:

kicked myself out of paradise
left a hole in the morning
no note no goodbye

the man I lived with
was patient and hairy

he cared for the animals
worked late at night
planting vegetables
under the moon

sometimes he held me
our long hair tangled
he kept me from rolling
off the planet

it was
always safe there
but safety

wasn't enough. I kept nagging
pointing out flaws
in his logic

he carried a god
around in his pocket
consulted it like

a watch or an almanac
it always proved
I was wrong

two against one
isn't fair! I cried
and stormed out of Eden
into history:

the Middle Ages
were sort of fun
they called me a witch

I kept dropping
in and out
of people's sexual fantasies

now
I work in New Jersey
take art lessons
live with a cabdriver

he says, baby
what I like about you
is your sense of humor

sometimes
I cry in the bathroom
remembering Eden
and the man and the god
I couldn't live with

The Coming of Lilith, Professor Judith Plaskow:

> Meanwhile Lilith, all alone, attempted from time to time to rejoin the human community in the garden. After her first fruitless attempt to breach its walls, Adam worked hard to build them stronger, even getting Eve to help him. He told her fearsome stories of the demon Lilith who threatens women in childbirth and steals children from their cradles in the middle of the night. The second time Lilith came, she stormed the garden's main gate, and a great battle ensued between her and Adam in which she was finally defeated. This time, however, before Lilith got away, Eve got a glimpse of her and saw she was a woman like herself.
>
> After this encounter, seeds of curiosity and doubt began to grow in Eve's mind. Was Lilith indeed just another woman? Adam had said she was a demon. Another woman! The very idea attracted Eve. She had never seen another creature like herself before. And how beautiful and strong Lilith looked! How bravely she had fought! Slowly, slowly, Eve began to think about the limits of her own life within the garden.

Lilith is a badass. A serious, serious badass. Lilith is the energy that surges through you and says, "No! No more!" You activate your inner Lilith the moment you say "No, I refuse to lie beneath you! I will not be ruled over by you!" You fully experience the power of Lilith in the energy of "I will not be shamed!"

You may shame me. But I will <u>not</u> be shamed.

Even the angels of God could not bring Lilith back, though they tried three times. She would not be moved.

Questions to Consider:

- *Try writing your own Lilith story. If you were wild and free, incorrigible and bold beyond measure, what would you do? What does "No! No more!" look like in your life?*

- *Have you ever stood your ground <u>no matter what?</u> For who? For what?*

- *How have you practiced self-advocacy?*

- *If you could found a national magazine based on your point of view at this particular time in your life, what would you name it?*

Strategy #4: Return to Sender

Know this: ALL the shame you carry you have absorbed from someone else's energy field. What does this mean? It means that your shame, which feels like the most intimate, personal part of you–so personal it feels obscene to expose it to anyone—is not even yours! And, even more than that: No matter what you did, no matter how perfectly good, obedient and amazingly pleasing you ever could have been, it would have made *absolutely no difference*. You could have been utterly rotten or a perfect angel, shame was still coming your way.

This is where the Garden of Eden story gets very interesting. Do you know where the tree with the forbidden fruit was located? Let me ask another way: If God did not want Eve to eat from the tree, where would be the best place for the tree to be located in the garden? Maybe way over to one side or tucked behind some gigantic spread of poison ivy to deter trespassers? But no! The tree was planted RIGHT IN THE MIDDLE OF THE GARDEN.

Let me bring this down to a personal level. I have a love/ hate relationship with Oreos. I love to eat them. I hate having eaten them. If God put an Oreo tree in the middle of the Garden of Eden and told me that I was forbidden to eat from it, I'd give myself a fifty-fifty chance…on a good day.

My point is this: It was a setup. The whole system was rigged against Eve. The punishment did not belong to her any more than the ridiculous "crime" of eating a piece of fruit. (A much healthier option, by the way, than Oreos!) The shaming of Eve was unavoidable. It had nothing to do with her. It belongs to the people who wrote the story. It also belongs to the people today whose agenda is to maintain the story. These people are not invested in your happiness or your well-being. They are not interested in growth, transformation, or even best practices. They want to maintain the status quo, which means maintaining their mythology.

I'm asking you to write another story. I'm asking you to release all the shame that lives in your energy field and send it back from whence it came.

As we consider shame as a result of absorbing someone else's energy, it becomes imaginable that we can release that shame, release that which was never ours in the first place, like a letter that was mailed to us but is not ours.

When you get a piece of mail that doesn't belong to you, what do you do? You write on the letter: *Return to Sender* and put it back in your mailbox to be picked up the next day. Imagine that letter is your shame. You've been holding onto it for so many years. It is time to practice how to "Return to Sender."

As you practice this, you'll get better and better at knowing how to sort your mail. You'll get better and better at identifying the letters that are not yours to open. And as your mail carrier (the Universe) is taught by you that you <u>do not</u> receive other people's mail, that mail just may stop coming altogether.

And how do you know if it's your mail?

If it's not kind, it's not your mail.

Remember: It is a federal offense to open mail that is not yours. Take all the mail that has come to you—all the words and the messages that you have absorbed that are not kind, all the energy that you are carrying that does not support your happiest, freest, most dazzling, peaceful, relaxed, inspired, Divinely lit-up life – then seal them up in envelopes (or burn them!) and Return Them to Sender!

Questions to Consider:

- **Is there something you have felt guilty for or "bad" about that you might let go of today?**

- **What did you used to feel guilty about that you no longer do? How have you grown?**

Strategy #5: Break the Taboo

I do not remember ever talking about shame or, for that matter, listening to anyone else talk about it, until I was in graduate school. In my home, my parents were very open. My father was an obstetrician and from the kitchen phone (attached to the wall at that time) I learned about cervix dilation, the uterus, and contractions. My mother was also very open and easy to talk to about anything that felt private. Yet, incredibly, the most private part of me, the part that I most needed to share in order to heal, I never spoke about. The adults in my life never talked about their shame either. I don't think we had any more shame than other people, but it was definitely there in all of us. It always is. No one gets through childhood without their fair share of shame. And no one talks about it. It's as if shame itself is as taboo as the things we're ashamed of.

Here we were, four people living together for two decades with shame driving so much of our pain and suffering and we were completely unconscious of it. There was yelling, crying, and blaming, followed by periods of relief; then we would all cycle through the drama again. This is how I grew up and, actually, I think it was rather normal (if normal is synonymous with common), but clearly suboptimal.

How much better would it have been if we talked about feeling ashamed and being hurt by each other or other people? How much better could it have been if we could have held each other, and ourselves, with conscious compassion?

> *"Out beyond ideas of wrongdoing and rightdoing, there is a field. I'll meet you there."*
> *~Rumi*

How might it have been different if my parents knew how to soothe the injured parts of themselves, and in me and my brother? How might it have been different if they had been aware of how parents transfer shame to the next generation? How would it have been different for all of us if we had been able to identify what shame even is and know that it is no one's fault? How might it have been different if we had been able, as Rumi suggests, to meet each other in the field with compassion, mercy and deep, deep love?

Questions to Consider:

- **What intergenerational patterns stand out to you in your family?**

- **How have you been affected by these patterns?**

- **Are there any patterns that you are determined to break?**

Strategy #6: There is Nothing Wrong with Me; I Just Need Time to Grow

When I first began to officiate weddings, right before the ceremony was about to begin, I would be stricken with terrible stomach cramps. The kind that, when in public, you have to grind your back teeth in order to get through.

One particular day I remember being in the bathroom just when the processional music began. (Note: It is not good to be the rabbi on the toilet when the processional music begins.) Somehow, I got myself together and glided in as seamlessly as a butterfly and cool as a cucumber. Nobody knew that I barely made it to the front of the room.

"Let us all stand for the receiving of the bride," I announced with just the right mix of authority and warmth in my voice.

Later, people said to me, "You are so calm. You bring such peace."

"Yeah, thanks. Bathroom?"

Shortly thereafter I called myself in for a serious talk:

Look, you have to find a way to manage your anxiety or find another occupation. You can't put yourself through this for the rest of your working life. And, eventually, it's gonna blow.

I decided to seek professional help. The therapist had a great silk scarf, sexy shoes and sat just right in her swivel chair.

"Simply put," she said after I told her my tale of gastrointestinal woe, "you are an anxious person. Some people are born anxious." She tilted her head ever so slightly. "Have you thought about medication?"

Now, I am in no way opposed to medication; however, I do take serious offense at being told that I was born an anxious person.

After that day, I made a decision: I was going to be a rabbi and I was not going to suffer debilitating anxiety. I was going to grow out of it. The problem was not that I was born anxious, the problem was that *I didn't trust myself.*

Slowly, slowly, I began to trust myself. The scene repeated many times:

1. Processional lines up
2. Bride comes out
3. Rabbi goes to bathroom
4. Music begins
5. Rabbi almost panics in bathroom
6. Rabbi comes out of bathroom
7. Ceremony begins
8. Ceremony is terrific!
9. Groom breaks the glass
10. Bride and groom kiss
11. Rabbi feels like she dodged another bullet

It took several years of "fake it till you make it" until one day I forgot to go to the bathroom. It didn't even occur to me to go; it was as if the bathroom didn't exist. I was absolutely secure in my being. I had learned to trust myself by walking the walk and talking the talk over and over again.

"Healing might not be so much about getting better as it is about letting go of everything that is not you - all the expectations - all the beliefs - and becoming who you are."
~Dr. Rachel Naomi Remen.

We can be so quick to let people in positions of authority label us. Don't let anyone do that to you. It's poisonous apple talk. And, please, don't limit yourself. If you are struggling with confidence, be patient with yourself and keep going. Sometimes it simply takes practice. One day you'll realize that what once gripped you so tightly and caused you so much suffering has, quite simply, slipped away. One day you'll realize that you are feeling quite extraordinary about just being you.

Questions to Consider:

- **How have you grown in the past decade or two?**

- **Are there things that you used to be afraid of that no longer scare you?**

- **Are there things that you used to worry about that no longer preoccupy you?**

Spiritual Exercise

My F*ing Fig Leaf

How Do You Wear Yours? Write down what comes to mind. (And please… feel free to rip this page out of the book and burn it!)

1. _____
   _____
   _____

2. _____
   _____
   _____

3. _____
   _____
   _____

4. _____
   _____
   _____

5. _____
   _____
   _____

Return to Sender

The Fourth Day

Letting in the Light

Women's March on Washington, January 21, 2017

"The wound is the place where the light enters you."
~Rumi

Coming Home to Yourself

I decided not to stay a member of the new temple. I just could not do the deep spiritual work that I longed to do there. I didn't feel at home there.

How I longed to feel at home!

I think *home* is a state of being that transcends place. It is the way you feel inside. Home is a feeling of inner safety and spaciousness. When I feel at home, I am relaxed and the furthest from feeling ashamed or afraid that I ever feel. I imagine that, biologically speaking, the feeling of being "at home" is linked to feeling physically safe from predators. But there are non-physical predators that threaten our peace of mind. Can they be faced and maybe even befriended? Is it possible to feel at home wherever I am? I wondered if I would ever feel at home in a specific congregation again. Maybe that was a good thing. Maybe it was possible to expand my spirituality to include all of humankind, even all life itself and to embrace life as my world temple.

"There is no need for temples,
no need for complicated philosophies.
My brain and my heart are my temples.
My philosophy is kindness."
~the Dalai Lama.

I needed to go at things alone for a while and see what it was like to allow myself to just be me without trying to fit myself into a category or label myself a certain kind of Jew. My spiritual journey felt private, requiring solitude and silence. I needed to face my inner demons and I couldn't do that in a congregational setting, because out in "public" I spent way too much time worrying about what other people thought of me.

I realized how much of my life I had spent looking for approval. Even though I was an outspoken feminist and grew up in an atheist temple, I still constantly checked the "Do You Like Me Meter." I could stand up for a cause, I could stand up for other people, but I could not really stand up for myself. I knew that learning how to do this was essential to my spiritual healing.

I yearned for all that is feminine—not necessarily female—but feminine in nature. I yearned for a place that was all-nurturing, all welcoming, all-loving. I needed a place where I didn't worry about being judged or being anything less-than. I knew there was no organization, congregation or community without its flaws. There were good teachers and I needed to find them, but there were no gurus. There were good practices and I needed to discover them, but there was no one perfect way. The place, the path, the way that I was looking for did not exist outside of myself. It could only be experienced from within. My spiritual journey turned inward because I needed to learn how to come home to myself.

One night at dinner my friend Jill shared, "I need to learn not to cry."

"What do you mean?" I asked. "Do you think you're too emotional?"

"No, not like that. I cry when someone confronts me. Like at work. I hate that. It's so embarrassing."

Jill is in her early thirties. I remember being in my early thirties when Rabbi Wine called me into his office for a talk. We sat chair to chair.

"Tamara," he told me, "you have to learn how not to cry. You can't let anyone see you lose your cool. You are the rabbi."

With that, I burst out crying. The point-of-no-return crying. The kind that leads to hyperventilation. Like Jill, I hated that about myself. It really was *so embarrassing*.

The cry was that of a very frustrated, ashamed, and scared little girl that lives in me. It was primal, the cry of an injured animal. She, above all, needed my love. I needed to literally return her breath to her.

In Hebrew, the word for spirit is *Ru-ach*. Ru-ach is also the word for breath and wind. It is the wind of the spirit that goes through us that gives us breath. Breathing is how the spirit moves through us. I felt the connection between becoming winded when I cried and losing spirit. I needed to return all that loss of spirit to myself.

Loving the frustrated, ashamed and scared child that lives in me became my spiritual practice.

Until I learned to take care of her, I would not feel at home anywhere in the world. But if I learned how to take care of her, I just might feel at home everywhere.

The Wounded Healer

I have a wooden bowl. It is the single most important object through which I tell my story and invite others to tell theirs. When I hold bereavement groups in my office, I place it in the center of the room. One Yom Kippur, the holiest day of the Jewish year, I spoke to the congregation with the bowl in my arms as a metaphor for what it means to live as a human being on this earth with compassion, dignity, power… and woundedness.

In the tortuous time after I resigned my pulpit, I placed the bowl on my nightstand, along with a creation by Kelly Rae Roberts, of a lovely woman wearing angel wings and balancing a bird's nest on her head. Across the woman's chest was written "Embrace Change," then down her body in beautiful fonts and colors: *Begin today. Surround yourself with good people. Surrender your fear. Feel the brightness of being alive. What is calling you? Take flight toward your dreams. Wear red shoes. Believe in possibility. Be brave.* For me, those words were prayers, psalms, incantations and inhalations. *"Be brave… Believe in possibility…"* I relied on them to work their magic as I lay in my bed and read them sideways because my head was too heavy to lift off the pillow.

I warred against the intrusive, excruciating thoughts about what happened and who said what and what I said and what I should have said and what I wish I had not said. The thought loops about the people who were the last people in the world that I wanted to think about just would not leave my head! *I should get them their own apartment*, I said to myself one night as I lay in bed reading the words of Kelly Rae Roberts, *maybe then they'd finally move out of my head!*

I would just lie there and grip the angel and bowl—both of which were placed strategically on my nightstand to face me—in my gaze and pray that I had the strength to continue to trust my truth. This went on for two years before I had the strength to move them. No one knew how fiercely I depended on those two objects to get out of bed in the morning.

The bowl—purchased by my mother while on a trip to Appalachia and shortly thereafter pirated by me—is oblong and stands about a foot tall. On one side, the grain of the wood is smooth as it spreads across the surface of the bowl. Viewing the object displayed from this side, it looks beautiful—perfect, in fact—and rather ordinary. From this side, the bowl could be any nicely- shaped, sanded, and polished wooden bowl among a thousand other nicely shaped, sanded and polished wooden bowls. But if you turn the bowl around to the other side, it becomes extraordinary.

"The dark does not destroy the light; it defines it."
~Brené Brown

My mother described to me her encounter with the artist, who told her that while most woodworkers look for a perfect piece of wood to make the most perfect piece of art, he looks for rotted wood —wood that others would discard as being unusable and ugly. He takes that rotted wood and fashions the rest of the bowl around it. This is what makes his designs surprising, intricate, and one of a kind. The rotted wood transforms the bowl into art. Seen from the side with the rotted wood that is integrated into the shape, the bowl comes alive and becomes multi-dimensional, rough and soft to the touch with contrasting grains that look like they hold all the days of the tree it was sourced from, both during and after the tree's life. Seen from this side, the bowl becomes a great storyteller, a bearer of secrets, dreams, and the telling of both burning and resurrection.

The hole in the bowl created because of the rotting wood is not only beautiful, interesting, and powerfully unique, it serves another purpose as well: It lets in the light. Healing begins by letting in the light, which is just another way of speaking your truth. If you can say it out loud, you have already begun the healing process.

So often, shame keeps us from exposing our wounds to the light. In the darkness, wounds cannot heal; they fester and become infected. But natural light is Divine and contains a healing power that begins a process of renewal. When you let in the light, you are signaling to the Divine, "Come heal with me."

You can do this incrementally, like slowly opening a curtain to let in the daylight, or you can flood the wound with light, like flipping on a light switch. Everyone has his or her own pace. The important thing is that you let the light in.

"The wound is the place where the light enters you."
~Rumi.

Silvia (whose name has been changed for confidentiality) was nearly ninety years old when she came to see me. She had never talked to a psychologist before. As I invited her to come inside and sit down, I wondered what this beautiful old woman needed that I might provide.

"What I am going to tell you," she began, "I have never told anyone, but I decided that I do not want to die without someone knowing." She was soft-spoken, but there was determination in her voice as she added, "This is very difficult for me."

I leaned forward and we took each other's right hand. I placed my left hand on top as if to say, *I am all in. I'm here to listen. You can speak when you are ready.* We sat like that for a minute or two, Silvia willing herself to continue and I resisting the urge to say anything more. I just held her hand and opened my breathing to make space for whatever needed to come next.

I could not imagine what came next.

Silvia began to recall the abuse she endured as a young bride, married to a much older man. She described years of being terrorized by this man and painted graphic descriptions of what she felt and saw as he committed murder in front of her—to warn her. She described the moment she decided to run for her life in Eastern Europe and escape to America. She eventually remarried to a loving man, had a family of her own and never spoke about her ordeal until that day in my office. Over the course of six weeks, Silvia came every Wednesday to tell her story to me.

These were the hardest sessions I have experienced in my career. Sometimes halfway in I had to refocus my mind on my own breathing and discipline myself to keep listening. *Inhale of breath, my diaphragm expanding; exhale of breath, air pushing and gliding along my throat. Expand, push, glide. Expand, push, glide.*

Listening is an act of love. It is the way we say to each other, "You matter." People often ask me what they should say to someone who has endured a tragic loss. My answer is simple: "Listen." Listening is more than hearing another's words; it is the act of paying attention to them. It is also deeply feminine. It is often the way a mother listens to her children that determines how they feel about themselves. The very moment you begin to listen deeply to another soul through the lens of love, you become a healer.

I listened for hours and hours until Silvia spoke absolutely all of it. And then something extraordinary happened: She began to smile. Gradually our sessions became lighter—more about the present. She focused on the challenges that she was having as she aged, and most of all, spoke about the love that is now in her life. She released the past into the present and at our last session she declared, "I feel free."

Silvia had let in the light.

According to oncologist and teacher of integrative medicine Dr. Rachel Naomi Remen, "Wounding and healing are not opposites. They're part of the same thing. It is our wounds that enable us to be compassionate with the wounds of others. It is our limitations that make us kind to the limitations of other people. It is our loneliness that helps us to find other people…"

Our wounds are our most precious treasure maps, showing us the way to the Divine. Although we would not choose them and with all our might seek to reject them, disguise them and deny them, they are truly our most loyal and direct living paths to wholeness. Our wounds are sacred portals to our deepest self. They deserve to be honored and revered. Far from ugly deformities, they are our greatest teachers and source for life. Indeed, knowing and loving our wounds is loving life in its rawest form. This is Divine work.

If you have been injured by life or by other people - if you know what it is like to truly be like Eve, down on your knees; if you have been so humbled by life that you no longer judge other people harshly in their pain - you are a wounded healer. If you feel compelled to make the world a more inhabitable place for all beings because you know what it feels like to be deeply hurt or deeply lost, you are a wounded healer.

In western mythology, Eve was the first one to feel shame, to be wounded. Because of this, **Eve was the first one to become real.** With her wounds, she crosses over the threshold to our world, where there are emotions. Although she experiences great suffering, she is now capable of a full emotional life. For this, she deserves to be celebrated and welcomed.

Far from a sinner, Eve is the first wounded healer.

Who do you regard as great? Consider that all great people who have changed the course of history for the better are wounded healers. If you are wounded, know that inside the center of your woundedness—where all the pain and shame live—lies the seed for your capacity to heal yourself, others, and the world. In honoring your wounds and seeing them for what they are—the seat of your compassion to show up in life as a healer—you will discover your power.

The pursuit of self-love and self-worth are a woman's most important endeavors.

I chose to speak about Eleanor Roosevelt at my Bat Mitzvah in part because she grew up feeling like an ugly duckling. This feeling of being an outcast, this wound, propelled her to fight for the right of every human being to live in dignity.

Consider that Mahatma Gandhi was also a master at using his wounds to effect change. On June 7, 1893, a young Gandhi sat down in a first-class railway compartment with his ticket. A white man objected and he was told to go to the back of the train. Gandhi refused and was forcibly removed from the train. This experience was a moment of awakening for Gandhi. It catapulted him forward into activism.

Gandhi was one of the greatest wounded healers who ever lived. Never was he more powerful than during the days when he refused to eat. Emaciated, physically dying, he moved an entire nation and changed the course of history. A man weighing well under a hundred pounds, his wasted body wrapped in a cloth, lifted up the entire world like Atlas. In his state of woundedness, he was the most powerful human being on planet Earth.

The Heroine's Journey

Long before any of the great knights from King Arthur's court set off on their quest for the Holy Grail, a woman named Eve began a quest to do the seemingly impossible: **After losing everything, she decided to find herself.**

Eve's journey is the heroine's journey. In her journey, she must overcome internal obstacles like shame, loneliness, despair, harsh inner voices and layers of negative conditioning. The heroine's reward is not external honor. Rather it is inner security and lightness of being. She is not looking for a trophy or a sacred object.

The heroine's journey is a quest for inner light.

Unlike the masculine hero who sets out on his journey at the height of his physical powers, riding high on horseback and ready to take on all opponents, the heroine begins her journey in a state of powerlessness and vulnerability. She is bereft, banished from life as it used to be and faced with the daunting task of finding another path. Think of Eve on the ground in that state of shameful nakedness. She has no high horse on which to ride; she must travel on foot and discover her capacity for endurance along the way. Whereas a man begins his quest confident that he can make it to the end, a woman aches with self-doubt. She thinks to herself, *Can I do this? Can I get through this?*

Every woman wants to be able to say, *"I did it! I made the journey, step by step. I have become my own person and I like who I am."* In light of the heroine's journey, let's reread the words of my beloved Grandma Jeanette from Chapter Two:

> *When I was a child there was no one there to say, "I love you,"
> or when I came home from school to ask me, "How was your
> day?" All my life I felt like I was climbing a tall wall. It was
> brick, that's how hard it felt. But I just climbed, step by step.
> Now at the end of my life, I can say to myself, "Jeanette, you*

did it! You climbed the wall!" It is such a good feeling. I climbed the wall and on the other side I discovered a secret garden. There are roses and peonies. This is my garden. I did it. I made it!

Can you feel that? That power! That bliss of finally, finally feeling powerful and worthy!

As women, the supreme value of life is to become our own heroines. This is what Maya Angelou meant when she titled the book that she wrote in her later years, *Wouldn't Take Nothing For My Journey Now.* She was claiming her heroine's journey, and nothing is sweeter, nobler, more worthwhile and more kick-ass!

After Paradise is lost to her, Eve journeys through three stages. Each stage carries certain energy and energetic opportunities. Each stage has its own realizations and callings. Each are equally deserving of honor. Each are noble passageways to knowing the Divine. These stages are non-linear and best thought of as phases of the moon, waxing, waning, emerging and rescinding, expanding and contracting. The stages are fluid and sometimes even overlapping. They can loop back on each other. They reflect every emotion that every woman experiences in the course of her lifetime—over and over again.

I believe that Eve can sense you. As your awareness of her increases, you will be able to sense her, too. Eve may come to you in a sudden clear knowing. She may come to you through your emotions as a flood of sadness or anger when you are defending your rights or the rights of anyone you love. You may become aware of her when you feel restless and anxious to get to another place in your life. Certainly, she is there in your loneliness. *Anytime your story aligns with Eve you have an opportunity to connect to her. Anytime you identify the themes in your life that you share with Eve and you claim your power in the story of your life—you are connecting with Eve.*

We heal in tandem with the Feminine Divine.

The Feminine Divine is actually asking us to be Her partner in healing and empowerment. We have an extraordinary opportunity to work with Her in tandem. As she heals, we heal. As we heal, she heals. We say to her, "We did not forget you" and by doing this we send a profoundly healing message to all the parts of ourselves that we judge harshly and seek to reject.

Here is the key: As you raise your vibration, as you move towards self-love, self-care, self-acceptance and self-worth—as you claim yourself as Divine, the collective energy of feminine light increases, too. As you ascend, Eve ascends. As you heal, the light of the Feminine Divine grows and more light is available in the feminine energy field.

Your healing, the healing of Eve, and all of feminine energy are interconnected in the most exquisite way.

From the time of The Fall (her descent) until the time of her rightful return of spiritual power and joy (her ascent) they are:

1. **Initiation:**

   This stage contains all the emotions that follow the initial loss of Paradise: shock, disorientation, and deep sadness. For the first time, Eve hears the sound of herself wailing. This phase represents the initial experience of every woman after major loss and life change: divorce, loss of a loved one or a job, illness or any other painful disruption that turns the world upside down.

   Eve can't seem to wrap her head around what happened. *Where is she?* She is down on her knees—literally. Sleep is her only refuge. But when she wakes up she doesn't know if she has the strength to get out of bed. Everything hurts. Everything requires great effort. Every bone in her body aches to go home.

She needs other people, nature, pets. Eve needs comfort and reassurance. She needs to reestablish basic safety. Eve, the Great Mother, needs mothering.

2. Awakening:

This is Eve's life after some time has passed since The Fall. She has survived Initiation and this is a formidable achievement! But she continues to experience great frustration, anger and sadness. Here is where we come in touch with our anger. But this is healthy anger. It fuels us to get going and move forward. It allows us the power to leave behind what no longer serves our highest good. In the Middle Stage, Eve is fully immersed in the grieving process. She is fighting to live. She knows that it has to get better. People move on—*don't they?* But how? When are you done grieving? How much longer? Anger, frustration, and irritability are all natural emotions during this time. Since Awakening requires a burst of energy, healthy anger helps energize Eve. She has a right to be angry. She has a right to feel frustrated and irritable.

As awful as this time is, there is a sense that something new is coming. Something she has never felt before is bubbling up inside of her. There are these flashes of hope that she feels whenever she realizes: I'm still here! I did not die! I'm actually doing it! This new sensation lighting her up is called *personal power.* As this power increases, she becomes curious about what the future might hold and a new emotion takes hold: *hope.*

3. Rising:

The day comes when Eve hears a strange sound, unrecognizable but at the same time almost familiar. She realizes that this is the sound of herself laughing! Eve is realizing things rapidly now, how much easier it is to go to sleep at night and get up in the morning, that she actually likes being with people, and that the trees outside her window, while not as grand as Eden, are a comfortable reminder of the beauty that is still around her.

Eve is proud of herself and kind of awestruck! Sometimes she even dares to think to herself, "I made it!" It's not that there aren't moments, even many moments, of deep sadness. She still cries easily and often. But she has learned how to carry her sadness with Grace. There is a certain feeling of poetic justice in her—a sense that she is coming full circle. This feeling of satisfaction is her greatest achievement. For the first time in her life she knows what it is like to experience personal empowerment.

This stage is the time when women can pool their light and make real change. This is the time for activism. Today, all over the United States, we refer to women as "rising." There is a shared feeling among women that we are entering the third stage of the heroine's journey.

Which stage calls to you? Which encompasses the profound emotional energies that you are experiencing at this time in your life? You are looking for places in your life's story where you align with Eve. This overlay—this connection between you and Eve—is the contact point for the Feminine Divine. This is where you will do your tandem healing.

Spiritual Exercise

Where Are You on Your Heroine's Journey?

Put a check next to the words that resonate strongly with you.

1. Initiation: Early Stage Eve

__feeling ashamed

__feeling abandoned

__feeling isolated

__feeling the shutdown of intuitive powers

__aware of harsh inner voice full of judgment

__feeling confused

__feeling disoriented

__feeling bereft

__feeling vulnerable

__feeling numb

__urge to withdraw and hide

__thinking: "This sucks!"

__persistent worry: "This is never going to get better."

__muddy thinking

> **If most of your energy is here, you are needed as one who allows herself to be loved and gives others the great gift of trust.**

2. Awakening: Middle Stage Eve

__longing for a world of wholeness

__longing to retrieve your joy

__longing for deep connection

__feeling enraged

__feeling awkward

__feeling irritable

__feeling restless

__feeling exhausted

__experiencing chronic pain

__thinking: "I'm not myself."

__emerging new intuitions

__urge to put aside time for personal care

__realizing: "I'm going through a big learning."

__aware that something better is coming

If most of your energy is here, you are needed to show up and tell the truth about your experience.

3. Rising: Mature Stage Eve

__experiencing flashes of "light at the end of the tunnel."

__feeling increased inner peace

__feeling joyful

__feeling energized

__being connected to your intuition

__spiritually engaged

__realizing: "I have something to teach."

__feeling empowered

__increased readiness to connect to other women

__thinking clearly

__ready for adventure

__feeling rich

__playfulness

__heightened creativity

**If most of your energy is here, you are needed
as a role model and way-shower!**

As you understand and embrace yourself as a heroine on her journey, you will be able to face whatever it is you are going through with power. You will come to see that whatever happens in your life is part of your heroine story. It may suck. It may hurt like hell. But you can take all the parts of your life—what you are proud of, ashamed of, and everything in between—and make it a *whole* story.

You will make yourself whole by seeing your life as a whole story.

The Fifth Day

Remembering Who We Once Were with the Mother God

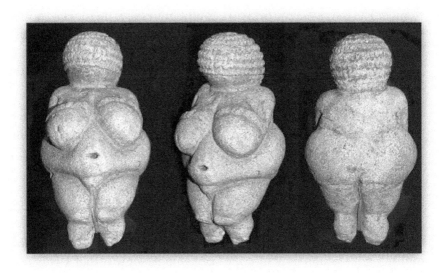

Woman of Willendorf Figure, 30,000 BCE. Discovered August 7, 1908, Austria

"How did it actually happen? How did men initially gain the control that now allows them to regulate the world in matters so vastly diverse as deciding which wars will be fought when to what time dinner should be served?"
~When God Was a Woman, Merlin Stone

Hypnotized by Patriarchy

*A*lmost compulsively, I began researching Eve and the Mother Goddess. Since I now knew beyond a shadow of a doubt that the Feminine Divine was real, I wondered: *Where is the actual evidence for Her?* I knew that I was meant, as we all are, to find my way back to Her.

I devoured every article, book, website and blog I could find; I looked at countless images of artifacts. I crossed deep rivers of patriarchy using the stepping-stones of intuition that had been laid by my great-great grandmothers and their great-great grandmothers. Here was an artifact found in Crete, there was another found in France. Here was a cave drawing found in France, there was another found in Turkey. As I was digging, imagining, reading and rereading, a truly awe-inspiring picture of Her began to emerge. In *When God Was a Woman*, Merlin Stone describes a similar experience:

> The more I read, the more I discovered. The worship of female deities appeared in every area of the world presenting an image of woman that I had never before encountered.

I'd always thought that what I knew about the past was pretty revolutionary. I mean, I was raised in a tribe of atheists who valued egalitarianism and skepticism! I thought this gave me a certain cutting, anti-establishment edge. But this new stuff that I was now learning and piecing together about what past cultures actually believed, what life was like for women and how God was understood—well, it was like discovering another galaxy.

It took time to deconstruct my assumptions about what life was like 5,000, 10,000 or 35,000 years ago. Step by step, layer-by-layer, a new understanding—beautiful, vibrant, sacred and begging to be reborn—came into light. *I was a spiritual archaeologist digging for my sacred past.* And what I discovered BLEW MY MIND.

What *was* life actually like for women 25,000 years ago? I think most people would say it's impossible to know, but most would guess it was probably much, much worse than today. After all, we are an evolving society. We invent things. We progress. So, it's fair to assume that women suffered far more in the past than today.

That is exactly what I thought! I had it that women's rights and the quality of our lives had moved forward in a linear fashion, that it had been a steady progression to the hard-won freedoms in the modern world. In other words, I believed that today was a vast improvement over the past.

Furthermore, I believed that men had always ruled and wielded power over women. *Maybe somewhere out there, somewhere on planet Earth,* there were exceptions—unusual African tribes or Native American men who actually respected women and "allowed" them their freedom. Yes, there were Cleopatra, Helen of Troy and Joan of Arc. Certainly, we can all name a half-dozen other examples of women who ascended to power and ruled. But I believed these were the rare exceptions to the rule.

Why?

Because like you, I am a product of a society that holds the collective understanding that *since men are physically stronger* and *women bear children,* men protected and, therefore, dominated women. Always. Like ever since we lived in caves. Furthermore, men were the ones who invented the tools to hunt, while women spent their time as domestic workers, preparing food and raising children. This theory reaches the natural conclusion that male dominance is a biological truth. All you have to do is visit a museum or open up a book of archaeology and there they are: a group of women sitting on the threshing floor with babies in hand while men hunt, fish, and make tools. This picture of prehistoric days has been reinforced in our books, movies and museums so many times that even I—a rebellious Jewish woman who is predisposed towards disobedience—missed it. I never imagined anything other than 200,000 years of men in charge.

Ugh.

In *The Great Cosmic Mother: Rediscovering the Religion of the Earth,* Monica Sjöö and Barbara Mor point out:

Men (and women) are still conditioned by all patriarchal political, religious, economic, and cultural institutions to believe that humanity is much better off now than we ever were in the dark, inchoate, and anonymous (read: female) past. But there was an era, before the patriarchal revolution took effect, when women and men cooperated in equality, producing and creating and worshipping together.

I'd been hypnotized by patriarchy. This extended to my conceptualization of God. I mean, obviously, on an intellectual level I knew that God did not have a gender. Yet I had nevertheless spent all my life imagining God as a man. In part, this is because Hebrew, the language of the Bible, has gender. The Hebrew words used for God barraged me with pronouns and images that were intentionally, and most definitively, male. God is "King," "Shepherd," "Father," "Lord," and "Master." God is never, "Mother." In Christianity, there is Mother Mary, but she is not God.

Add to this the pervasive myth that man is made in God's image and woman is only made from a part of man, and you will see emerging a very clear pecking order with woman at the bottom:

God.

Man.

Woman.

So, while everyone insisted that "He" was invisible, "He" never seemed invisible to me.

"Man made God in his own image."
~Eckhart Tolle.

In my mind's eye, I pictured God as Michelangelo and billions of other people pictured him: with a long white beard and an outstretched hand.

Well, this must always have been the case, I reasoned. *This was*

100

the case from the beginning of time until the 1960s when feminists burned their bras and repainted the chapel ceilings. God became a woman in the 1960s.

Yep, I'll admit it. That's what I imagined up until very recently.

My understanding of the distant past was based upon three faulty conclusions:

1. Men always dominated women because men are physically stronger.

2. The further you go back in time the worse life gets for women.

3. God was male since the beginning of time.

But in actuality…

1. Many, many societies prior to 3000 BCE practiced matrilineal descent. These societies, which were among the most populated and developed places in the world, also saw God as a woman. (Note: BCE and CE are alternatives to BC and AD. BCE stands for "before common or current era.")

2. In these societies, there was high regard for the female. Women owned property, inherited property, conducted business, and led public worship. There were laws that protected them in cases of rape and they could, if they chose, divorce their husbands.

3. The Goddess was the procreator and protector of all. Since the Goddess was understood to be the source of all life, so was a woman's body, which was considered sacred.

In *When God Was a Woman*, Merlin Stone discusses the surprises that Greek historian Diodorus Siculus wrote about in 49 CE after encountering women-oriented societies in Northern Africa:

> All authority was vested in the woman, who discharged every kind of public duty. The men looked after the domestic affairs just as the woman do among ourselves and did as they were told by their wives. They were not allowed to undertake war service or to exercise any function of government or to fill any public office, such as might have given them more spirit to set themselves up against the women. The children were handed immediately after birth to the men who reared them on milk and other foods suitable to their age.

For a deeper understanding of what once was and what came to be, let's look at three areas of primary concern to women. Pay attention to the dates and how things changed through time once patriarchy took hold.

Rape:

In 2000 BCE in Sumer (Southern Iraq), if a man raped a woman he was put to death; however, by 1250 BCE in Assyria, if a man raped a woman then the husband or father of that woman was to rape the rapist's wife or daughter and/or marry his own daughter to the rapist. By 400 BCE, according to Hebrew Law, a raped woman must be put to death if she was already married or betrothed.

Per Biblical law: An unmarried woman could be compelled to marry her rapist, as long as the rapist could pay the standard bride price and the woman's father consented to the marriage. (Deuteronomy 22:28–29).

Marriage and Infidelity:

In 2300 BCE Mesopotamia, women took two husbands. (Note: Mesopotamia is located within the Tigris-Euphrates river system and was the first river valley civilization.) In 2000 BCE, in the

Sumerian State of Eshnunna (Mesopotamia):

- Permission for marriage was required by both mother and father.

- If a man had a child with another woman or took another wife, he could be forced out of his house without any of his possessions.

- A man who took a second wife after his first wife had given birth was expelled from the house without any of his possessions.

- If a woman had a child with another man while her husband was away at war, when he returned, he was expected to take her back as his wife without any punishment.

- Women were engaged in business activities, held property in their name, fully participated in all religious rites, and lent money.

In 1754 BCE, per the Code of Hammurabi:

- If a woman committed adultery she was to go to the temple, take an oath and return home to her husband without punishment.

- Women were free to divorce.

- Seven of Hammurabi's Laws were concerned with the priestess of the temple and her right to inherit.

Love poems discovered in Egyptian tombs suggest that it was the woman who did the courting. This is a sharp contrast to Biblical law, which states:

"If, however, the charge is true and no proof of the girl's

virginity can be found, she shall be brought to the door of her father's house and there the men of her town shall stone her to death. She has done a disgraceful thing in Israel by being promiscuous while still in her father's house. You must purge the evil from among you." (Deuteronomy 22:20-21)

Religious Authority:

The world was full of female Gods. For example, Nut was said to have created all that is in being. It was the goddess Nut that first placed Ra, the sun God, into the sky. Other texts tell of Hathor, who took the form of a serpent. Isis wore wings, invented agriculture, was a healer, a physician and established laws of justice in the land.

However, by 3000 BCE male deities were introduced by the Indo-Europeans who conquered Babylonia. Their God Marduk murdered the Goddess to gain supreme power in Babylon. This same myth is told in different areas of the Near East, though the God has different names.

By the time of the eighteenth Dynasty, women in Egypt were no longer part of the clergy and served only as temple musicians.

By the end of the 2nd millennium BCE, Babylonian women could no longer engage in business affairs without the permission of their husbands.

Biblical law states:

"But if her husband nullifies them [her vows] when he hears about them, then none of the vows or pledges that came from her lips will stand. Her husband has nullified them…" (Numbers 30:12)

"Do not allow a sorceress to live." (Moses speaks in Exodus 22:18)

The New Testament states:

"Let a woman learn in silence and full submission. I permit no woman to teach or to have authority over a man; she is to be silent. For Adam was formed first, then Eve, and Adam was not deceived, but the woman was deceived and became a transgressor. A woman will be saved through childbirth if she remains in faith and love and sanctification with modesty." (1 Timothy 2:15, New Testament)

"For the man is not of the woman, but the woman of the man. Let the woman keep silence in the churches, for it is not permitted unto them to speak; but they are commanded to be under obedience, so saith the law. And if they learn anything, let them ask their husbands at home; for it is a shame for the woman to speak in the church." (I Corinthians 11:2, 7, 9)

The Talmud states:

"...and do not converse excessively with a woman. They said this even about one's own wife; surely it applies to another's wife. Consequently, the sages said, 'Anyone who converses excessively with a woman causes evil to himself, neglects Torah study, and will eventually inherit Gehinnom (hell)." (Pirkei Avot: Chapters of The Fathers 1:5)

"The more wives, the more witchcraft." (Pirkei Avot: Chapters of The Fathers 2:8)

By the time the Hebrew Bible was canonized, women had been effectively shut out from religious authority and power in the community. In Judaism, women were (and still are among many Jewish communities) forbidden to even touch the Torah, let alone read from it. In 313 CE, the Roman Emperor Constantine declared Christianity the official religion of the Roman Empire. In doing this, he spread the patriarchy throughout the world along with Roman power and influence. By 391 CE the worship of idols and Paganism became illegal with deathly consequences and in 500 CE the last Goddess temple was closed.

Women's stories and women's ways began to disappear. As men were taught to remember and write down their stories, women were taught to forget their experiences and be silent. For thousands of years, very few women learned to read and write. The pervasive cultural understanding was that if something really happened, a man would witness it. A woman's point of view was at best, useless, and at worse, poisonous.

As the years went by, God seemed to belong more and more to men. God seemed more and more to be a man, too. Women seemed more and more... well, like women who were born second-class citizens and always at least one step removed from the Creator.

The Missing Queen of Heaven

God in the feminine did not just disappear, however. The Hebrew Bible can be read as a testimony to how incredibly difficult it was to convince people to let go of the Mother God and accept the new Father God.

In the Hebrew Bible, the name for the Mother God is *Asherah* or *Queen of Heaven.* As you read the Bible, you continuously read descriptions about how the people, "Made Asherahs or Asherah poles" at "High Places." The High Places were usually located on hilltops or in groves and always involved sacred trees. In all, there are forty-four such references—all of them directives to the people to stop worshipping the Mother God. In fact, the Bible says that if you come upon any of these High Places, you must,

> "Break down their altars, smash their sacred pillars and burn their Asherah poles in the fire; cut down the idols of their gods and erase the names of their gods."

> (Deuteronomy 12:3)

References to Asherah are everywhere in the Bible, from its beginning in the Book of Genesis to Chronicles, when it closes some 3,500 years later. In Deuteronomy, Jeremiah, Chronicles and Kings, the people who worship feminine religion absolutely enrage the establishment and even divide families. Specifically, many of the kings and their mothers worship Asherah. King Hezekiah publicly condemns his own mother, who prays to Asherah despite his warning. Jezebel loves Asherah and has four hundred prophets on the royal payroll worshipping with her. Actually, all the biblical queens practiced female religion, as did King Solomon, who had the audacity to put an idol in the image of an Asherah inside the great temple in Jerusalem! (Kings 1:18)

The narrator of the Book of Kings, who is a monotheist, distinguishes between a "good king" and a "bad king" by what the king does when it comes to Asherah. A good king seeks to destroy the Asherah religion, as is this account, "He broke in pieces the sacred pillars and cut down the Asherim (plural for Asherah) and filled their places with human bones." (2 Kings 23:14)

What is absolutely fascinating and inspiring is the strength of the resistance among the biblical Hebrews and Israelites to abandon Asherah. Even though they were warned and intimidated, they worshipped Her, "On every hill and under every tree." (1 Kings 14:23)

I'm naming this the first act of spiritual disobedience on record.

Why? Why did the Hebrews and Israelites refuse to give Her up? Why was it so difficult to convince them to accept the Lord? Because they needed Her. Because they loved Her. Because just like so many of us feel today, God makes no sense without Her.

Time after time, the Hebrews and Israelites went to their High Places. For it was there, amongst the trees and groves, that they felt Her spirit, there that they carved wooden poles and burned incense to talk to Her. They asked to be protected and nourished. They fashioned snakes there that represented Her power to know all the secrets of life and carved lions because She was the insurmountable, supreme force of nature. They prayed for women to be protected in childbirth. They prayed for babies to survive. They prayed for those who were sick to be healed. They prayed for the end of suffering. They prayed for rain and food. They prayed to be protected from their enemies. They prayed for the spirits of their ancestors. They brought all their sorrow and all their joy to Her. And they felt that their prayers were heard. She heard them. She protected them. She loved them as their Supreme Mother. *How could they have a full spiritual life without Her?*

In the same way our own mothers are not replaceable, they knew that the spirit of the Great Mother was not replaceable. They knew that a Father God was never going to be enough; they knew that without Her, there would be no truly fulsome, whole divinity.

The notion of God without the feminine would always be incomplete. So they refused to give Her up.

Make no mistake, it's not just women who revered Her. The prophet Jeremiah wrote an account of what he observed as families went to their High Places and how these acts of worship provoked God to be very, very angry:

> The children gather wood, the farmers light the fire and the women knead the dough and makes cakes of bread for the Queen of Heaven. They pour out drink offerings to other gods and provoke me to anger. The Lord declared, 'But am I the one they are provoking? Are they not rather harming themselves to their own shame?' (Jeremiah 7:18-19)

Years later, all Goddess worship was labeled paganism and "early" religion. In other words, the people who worshipped at the High Places were practicing fake, early religion because nothing was real until God became the Father.

I now realize that what Judeo-Christianity calls "Pagan," was really "female religion." The war on the pagan was essentially a war on the female. Pagans weren't worshipping "idols." They were honoring the feminine. "Those pagan idols had breasts," points out Merlin Stone.

Furthermore, the Pagans were not unenlightened people who lacked the spiritual sophistication to embrace monotheism. They were wise, intuitive, and loving people whose spiritual life was symbolized in the veneration of the Goddess of the Universe, The Queen of Heaven and the Creator of Life. The people in the Bible who built altars and made poles were our Divine sisters! They were celebrating life passages, praying for rain, food and protection. They were honoring life and time as it waxes and wanes with the moon and flows through the monthly cycle of a woman's body. They were honoring the female, and that's what was so damn threatening.

The brutal, biblical campaign against the "Pagans" was really a war against female power.

I never really got it—the intensity and the calamity of the constriction—how women and women's ways were literally smashed out by history. I knew men had power. I knew men wrote down the Bible but I didn't recognize the war on anyone who made idols and how their ways were erased. I didn't know to listen to a silence so vast, so stunning and so pervasive that it was actually shocking. There were thousands of years of silence.

Recently I published an article about Eve and the #MeToo movement, and I can tell you firsthand that there are a lot of people who do not like it when you, "Mess with the Bible." I received hundreds of comments, emails and several phone calls from men and women, Christian and Jewish, who accused me of being, "evil, poisonous, deceptive and stupid." A very popular commentator picked up the story and did an entire show on "Debunking Rabbi Kolton," which was viewed by 350,000 people. I was amazed by the backlash! My kids, who were a bit frightened, pointed out to me that this is more than enough people to fill several football stadiums. And the words that the commentator and the others used to describe me? They were the same words used to describe Eve.

Let me say emphatically, I'm *not* against the Bible. I'm certainly not against God. I'm for God. I'm rooting for God! I want God to be expansive and awesome! I need for God to be that way. But "The Lord" will not quench my spiritual thirst. I hear the silence and I miss Her too much. I hear the silence and I need Her too much. The absence of God as Mother is so loud, it's deafening.

I had awakened to an eerie truth: All I really knew about the distant past was *his* version. History was literally, *his* story, which to me means that history is at best half true.

I'm Rabbi Tamara Kolton and I'm here to report a crime: Half of all stories have gone missing.

For a long, long, time no one believed that there were any stories to tell before the written word. After all, since God was created with "The Word," there wouldn't really be anything worth telling anyway. This meant God was exactly 5,000 years old.

That's how it is today in America in almost every place of worship. If you go there, you will encounter a very young God.

But this book is a treasure hunt for *her*-story.

It is about retrieving those long-lost stories that belong to us. It's about uncovering a new version of prehistory based on tangible evidence that turns all our assumptions and theories about "biological truths" topsy-turvy-upside-down.

I'm going to spin you a different tale. I'm here to tell you that, yes, God is a young man. But God is also an old woman. A very, very, old woman.

Would you like to meet her?

The Seated Mother Goddess

In 1961, while digging at the site of a prehistoric city called Catal Huyuk (pronounced Cha-Tyl Hi-Yook), European archaeologists made an astonishing discovery. Catal Huyuk is located in what was Anatolia 8,000 years ago and today is Turkey and Crete. The site had never been excavated, making it a treasure chest just waiting to be opened.

There, inside a grain bin, archaeologists discovered a small clay figure, less than eighteen inches long. She became known as "The Seated Mother Goddess."

She is a figure of a very large woman, sitting soundly on a throne that is flanked by two twin lions. She appears to have given birth because there is a small round figure between her legs. Her breasts, stomach, thighs and buttocks are enormous. Each knee has a dimple, making it appear oversized and the same dimple appears across her abdomen. Although the figure is small, there is something massive about her. Her breasts sag like two rivers of flowing milk and seen from the rear, her buttocks go on forever, spreading behind her to match the rump of the lions on her left and right. Her shoulders are broad and she takes up the entire throne so that her seat fuses together with her flesh, giving us the impression that she could be riding the throne like a chariot, carried by lions.

Here is a photo of The Seated Mother Goddess from several angles:

Who is she? Many people formed many theories. Is she an ideal in a society of famine? Or maybe just a typical large woman of the time? Scientists looked to the bones found in nearby graves to understand. The analysis revealed that the women, men and children of Catal Huyuk ate a balanced diet, were trim and healthy. So, no, she was not a reflection of a typical woman of the time and no, she was not an ideal, because the people weren't hungry.

James Mellaart, the archaeologist who discovered her, explains her significance: "The statue allows us to recognize that the main deity worshipped by the people of Catal Huyuk was a Goddess."

Professor Anne Baring agrees. In her groundbreaking book, *The Myth of the Goddess*, Baring writes, "Long ago, 20,000 years ago and more, the image of a goddess appeared across a vast expanse of land stretching from the Pyrenees to Lake Baikal in Siberia. Statues in stone, bone and ivory, tiny figures with long bodies and falling breasts, rounded motherly figures pregnant with birth, figures with signs scratched upon them—lines, triangles, zigzags, circles, nets, leaves, spirals, holes—graceful figures rising out of rock and painted with red ochre—all these have survived through the unrecorded generations of human beings who compose the history of the human race."

Who is she?

The Seated Mother Goddess is how people imagined God 8,000 years ago. She is the Goddess who ruled Heaven and Earth and she is evidence of a distant past when women were sacred. Since her discovery, hundreds more figures have been found, making it clear, beyond a shadow of a doubt, that for the people of Catal Huyuk, God was a woman.

When I first saw a photo of "The Seated Mother Goddess," I did not think she looked like God. Honestly, she looked like my worst fear—the sagging, obese female form that I might become and that secretly, much of the time, feel I already am. She looked like the me that I try to hide, every crevice and fold that I secretly hate about myself. She looked disgusting. She looked like the kind of woman that we all reject and judge as gross.

For months, I struggled with her image. *This is the Mother Goddess? This is the Divine? She is so... fat. She is so... old. She is so... not sexy.*

And then it occurred to me: *The women of Catal Huyuk didn't hate their bodies.*

I am so saddened to realize the truth that as a woman, I feel so much more like Eve than The Seated Mother Goddess. I know so little about what it is like to sit tall, naked and glorious like her. I know only how to sit like Eve.

What was the first thing that Eve felt after she fell from Grace? Shame. Shame and self-hate. What did Eve hate? She hated herself. She hated her body, so she reached for a fig leaf to cover up her

112

nakedness. That's what gave her away—the fig leaf. God demanded, "Why are you wearing that?"

But He already knew.

If Eve could have spoken, if the words could have come out of her strangled voice, I think she would have said, "Because I hate my body."

Falling in Love with Catal Huyuk

I'm not really a nostalgic person. I don't look back and wish I could live my life all over again. Be back in high school? Middle school? Relive my childhood? No thank you. I'm not at all interested in going back to the time before I was born, either. I don't imagine that it was better back in the fifties or sixties. Drugs and rock n roll? Sexual experimentation and LSD? Thanks, I'll pass. Actually, I never imagined that it was better in the past at any time or in any era, especially for women. I like owning my own land in the suburbs of Michigan and I prefer not to be ruled over by my son and husband. I need my thyroid medication and I really like indoor plumbing.

So how surprisingly out of character it was to find myself longing for the past and in such a visceral way. Deep in my belly where all my longing lives, I ached to go back in time. Way back. Because it had become absolutely clear to me that there were societies in the distant past that knew what I've never known: God as a woman.

Just Imagine...

Imagine a place on the banks of a flowing river filled with ceremony and celebration. See how the people there are nourished by art, banquets, dance, processions and games that celebrate the seasons of life. Imagine a place free of violence. Imagine a society in which women and men are equally respected. Imagine spirituality constructed around the sacred nature of a woman's body. Imagine a time when all the curves and crevices of the feminine form were held as sacred because in her fluidity and fecundity, the community recognized God.

I've never heard of a place on Earth like it. As I describe it, don't be surprised if you, too, find yourself willing to give up all the comforts of modern life to go back in time and live there.

Catal Huyuk, located in modern-day Turkey, is known as one of the oldest towns in the world. Initial radiocarbon testing estimated that the city was founded in 6500 BCE; however, when archaeologists performed dendrochronology (the counting of tree rings) they realized that Catal Huyuk was probably settled earlier—around 7500 BCE. It is not known why the city was abandoned around 5700 BCE; however, the evidence suggests that this beautiful, highly advanced civilization thrived peacefully for 1,800 years.

The people lived on two mounds (indeed, the word catalhöyük means "forked mound" in Turkish) that were once connected by a channel of the flowing Çarşamba River. The clay in their soil was exceptional for agriculture and they grew many varieties of food, which made their diet well-balanced with vegetables, nuts and meat.

Additionally, the town is not a fortress. Far from it. In fact, if the Greeks had gone back in time to access the location they would have been horrified. Catal Huyuk had no strategic significance; it was chosen simply because it was beautiful.

What's more, archaeologists discovered that the town was scrupulously clean. There was very little rubbish in the buildings and there were separate areas outside for sewage and waste. They also found evidence of one other thing that happens when women are allowed to do what we love to do: a lot of redecorating.

Inside each home there were murals on the walls, depictions of life and dancing to honor the Great Mother. Archaeologists think that these were painted and repainted as often as once a month. Bulls were the major source of meat and their horns were used for decoration, marking the entranceways. To me, the houses look very Southwest, similar to Georgia O'Keeffe's home in New Mexico. Based on the archaeological findings, here are some photos of what the houses would look like if they were restored:

Catal Huyuk didn't have streets. Instead, people used connecting rooftops. This was possible because the houses were built close together like honeycombs. Each home had a ladder up to the roof, where all village life took place. This created a tight-knit community and protected the people. Communal ovens were found on the rooftops and what we would call plazas today.

The burial customs of Catal Huyuk portray a loving, intuitive community of people who were sensitive and kind. When a person died in Catal Huyuk they were buried beneath the home of the people they loved. This meant that in Catal Huyuk the people literally slept with their dead. In the grave, the body was placed in a fetal position. This way the person was returned to God in the same position in which he or she had been born; they were also ready for rebirth.

Children were always buried with their mothers, indicating that lineage passed through the female line. For every one child born alive, a child died during birth. These children were buried in such a way that when their mother died, they would be face to face with her and thus reunited.

As a rabbi, I am often asked when a loved one is dying, "What should I do?" As husbands and wives, children and even parents, peer into the abyss of loss from which we are bound inextricably. "Love her out of the world," is what I say and I mean it with all my heart and soul.

Just as we were loved into the world, we are meant to be loved out. Just as we came into the world, so do we go out. We came into the world in the fetal position and how right as rain that this is how we should leave.

In our culture, we often see birth and death as two separate times of life, one at the beginning and one at the end. But we are not meant to be linear beings. We are meant to flow in circles like the Goddess, to know cycles, seasons, many deaths and many rebirths.

When we lost God in the feminine, we lost the ability to live the sacred circle that is life.

Consider how death reflects birth and dying mirrors birthing— each will happen to all of us and we have very little control over how. Moreover, a pregnant mother knows that her baby will be born but she cannot tell you exactly when, just as the dying man who lays in a hospital bed with metastasized cancer knows he is going to die but he cannot give you the precise day and time, either. And the rest of us? Suspended somewhere between birth and death, we can only bear witness, help each other suffer less and live better, and when the time comes, let ourselves be loved out of the world, too.

When it is my turn, I shall want to remember what I learned from the precious people of Catal Huyuk and request to be folded back into the fetal position.

If all of this does not make you want to live there, here is the most amazing thing about Catal Huyuk. In all the unearthing by archaeologists, including twelve layers of twelve different cities, and taking into account the large population (with an average of 5,000 inhabitants Catal Huyuk was the most populated town of its time next to Jericho), *no evidence was found to indicate that this society ever went to war.*

Not ever.

Like not in eighteen hundred years ever.

No battle or violent siege is depicted anywhere on all those ever-changing murals in all those houses. Not a trace. The bodies buried there are intact, with no sign of trauma. Archaeologists found many, many tools but no weapons. They found jewelry, home décor and lots and lots of figures of The Mother Goddess, but they never found anything at all to indicate that there was any violence inflicted on or by the people of Catal Huyuk.

I wonder: *What will future civilizations learn from analyzing our gravesites and excavating our cities?* The question naturally arises: Will there be anything left of us to excavate? Will there be a civilization 9,000 years from now that is able to inhabit planet Earth? Will what we leave behind be so toxic that no scientist dare dig it up? And if they do, what will they think of us when they come upon the horrors of what we have done to each other and all our mass graves?

Imagine that instead of us analyzing the graves of Catal Huyuk, the people of Catal Huyuk were to analyze ours?

What would they make of even our most pristine cemeteries like Arlington? I think they would kneel on the mowed grass, staring row after row at the stark white markers, and weep. They would weep for all that we did not know and for who we could not be. This chilling truth is what drives this book. **We are a race who is racing to destruction. But it doesn't have to be this way. We can pivot. And the Mother Goddess will help us.**

Crete is another powerful example of a peaceful, woman-oriented society that thrived for a very long time. As Monica Sjöö, and Barbara Mor write in *The Great Cosmic Mother: Rediscovering the Religion of the Earth*, "The Cretans appear to have been gentle, joyous, sensuous and peace-loving. From the evidence of ruins, they maintained, like the Maltese Islanders, at least one thousand years of culture unbroken by war."

In July 2012, Catal Huyuk was named a UNESCO World Heritage Site. Today, archaeologists are actively excavating the site and regularly update their findings on YouTube.

From 1864 to 2008, from France to Crete, to the Pyrenees Mountains and as far as Siberia, Goddess figures were found in nearly every culture and society going back to the Ice Age. The Seated Mother Goddess is only one of hundreds of figures that were unearthed over the past 150 years. In fact, Lithuanian-American archaeologist Marija Gimbutas puts the number of artifacts unearthed, including pieces of pottery and painted caves, at more than 100,000.

In a time when few people traveled and when there was no communication from one side of the world to another, it is mind-blowing to realize that people who knew nothing of each other's cultures were creating the same forms of the female figure!

Constance Tippett is a sculptor who researched the feminine figures for thirteen years and now sculpts replicas of the forms. In discussing her work, she refers to the appearance of threads: "Threads are images that have similar characteristics that weave their way through time and appear on similar images in different civilizations."

Here are some examples:

- Women as keepers of the hearth
- The moon, and how women's bodies may have taught humans to count and conceive of time
- Women Goddesses and animals: birds, cats and lions, cows, snakes and scorpions.

Consider this in light of:

- Eve and the snake
- The Seated Woman and her lions
- The mythology of Cat Woman

- Mother Goose
- The Scorpion Woman who is known as "The Black Widow"
- The sign for medicine: two intertwined snakes, which were originally associated with healing and the feminine.

The excavations continue to this day. Most recently, in 2008, a six-centimeter statuette was discovered in a cave in Germany. Her large belly, breasts and thighs were carved out of a mammoth's tusk 35,000 years ago.

They are luminous, fluid, feminine figures sculpted out of mammoth bones, limestone and fired clay. And although they are obviously still, to my eyes they appear to be moving. They seem alive. Along with cave drawings, they are considered the earliest form of art discovered by anyone on Earth. And they are feminine forms.

I imagine Mother Earth giving birth to each figure and the scientists who assisted to be like midwives in the middle of the birthing process. I imagine how the body of Mother Earth opened slowly, painstakingly, and the luminous, strange creatures emerged one by one over the course of two hundred years into the light. Some emerged in the breach position, one tiny leg first to appear. Some were born on their sides or backs and slipped out of the earth more effortlessly. Like newborn babies, each figure required the care of human hands in the birthing process and needed to be meticulously cared for, cleaned, dried, wrapped in a soft cloth and placed in a cradle.

They also came out needing to be understood.

"Archaeological materials are not mute," says Marija Gimbutas. "They speak their own language. And they need to be used for the great source they are to help unravel the spirituality of those of our ancestors who predate the Indo-Europeans by many thousands of years."

In 1864, Paul Hurault, the Victorian archaeologist who made the first discovery, named the female figure, "The Immodest Venus," in reference to the Roman goddess of beauty. Since then, all the female figures, including The Seated Mother Goddess, are collectively known as "Venus figurines." The name is based on the assumption that all the figures represent an ancient ideal of beauty.

In the 1960s and 70s women began to challenge male assumptions about the figures. This is what Jill Cook, Curator of The British Museum, has to say:

> During a lecture on cave art, a wonderful sculpture flashed across the screen and our lecturer said, 'And we all know what Paleolithic men were thinking about when they made this!' And that was all that this wonderful piece of sculpture was going to get. And I have a problem with that. When I actually went out to look at these figures, which are between 20,000 and 30,000 years old, I realized that they represent women in all stages of their lives... They didn't seem to me to offer the posture or gaze of a classical Venus. If you think of beautiful sculptures of Venus rising from her bath, she directly connects with 'Him.' In attempting to cover herself, she actually accentuates her breast. That's an erotic piece. These ladies (Venus figures) have downward gaze. They are not trying to give you the come on. Their arms are tucked in on the swollen belly and their knees are always clenched together. (YouTube The Female Gaze in Ice Age Art. The British Museum. March 19, 2013.)

No, the figures weren't representations of beauty. They weren't fertility symbols either. They were images of our Divine Mother. They ARE images of our Divine Mother, and She is still talking to us.

"At the very dawn of religion," writes Merlin Stone, "God was a woman. Do you remember?"

Venus of Hohle Fels. Carved out of mammoth ivory, 35,000-40,000 years old. Discovered in 2008, Germany.

Venus of Willendorf. Carved in limestone 30,000 years ago. Discovered in 1908, Austria.

Venus of Dolni. Made of ceramic 29,000-25,000 years ago.
Discovered in 1925, Czech Republic.

Venus de-Laussel, Painted with red ochre and carved into limestone
25,000 years ago. Discovered in 1911, South-Western France.

Minoan Crete Goddess. Made of ceramic in 1700-1400 BCE. Discovered in 1903, Crete.

The Virus of Patriarchy

I went to see Lori. (You may remember Lori from Chapter One. Lori is a shamanic medium and a dear friend.) I sat down on her blue couch and with some trepidation asked, "Is it at all possible to ask to talk to Eve?"

This felt really bold. I mean, actually calling on Eve to come through and answer my questions?

"You want the spirit of Eve to come through?" Lori asked.

"Yes, I want to ask her how she lost her power. I want to know more about her energy, feminine power and how we got to patriarchy."

"Hold on," Lori responded, then she got quiet for a while. This is what she said next: "Eve is a consciousness... The story of Eve is mythological but the soul of Eve is in all of us." She continued, speaking now in first person for Eve:

"I am the woman of women.

I am the woman of all

But I am in all life form.

I am in the human life form

And non-human life form.

I am the essence of light that is feminine.

I am truth and wholeness.

There is no 'Is' without me.

All that 'Is' includes me.

There is no 'Suchness' without the suchness of female light.

"There was a fragmentation of light, when the fragmentation occurred one of the illusions that manifested was the concept of 'Us and Them.' The fragmentation of consciousness grew male and female. These ideas do not exist beyond the limitations of the mind. 'I' exist in the eternal I.

The story began long ago, though many, many, many people did not adopt the story.

I have been alive and well in the belly of many, many men and women for thousands of years who carried me with hopefulness, respect, love and honor.

Then there was torment. A shadow befell the Earth. When the shadow came and was allowed to persist it became a virus, a toxin in the mind of humanity. Though not all people were infused with this toxin, it did lead people astray. Many cultures began to exclude women, and men, but mostly women and girls. And mass hysteria became evident. Not all of this is written in history. It was as though a disease befell the Earth."

She then showed Lori how it entered in, came down and spun around the Earth.

"She is showing me an energy," Lori explained, "That came down over the Mediterranean and entered like a virus in the matrix. The virus spread in the system down through Africa, Asia, through China and wrapped around the Earth, permeating and then going into the West. She is showing me that the Aboriginal people and Shaman people did not get infected. There are beings that never got infected. But once it took hold it began a very strong 'Us vs Them' fight in the human consciousness. One by one cultures began to adapt a mythology of male power or male righteousness.

"Let me be very clear, women embodied the symbol of fertility, nurturance and sacred goddess holiness. It didn't self-destruct. It was a destructive force which came in. It was subtle—subtle shifts in consciousness became the destruction of the female sacredness but it accelerated once there were more formal religious organizations. Then it got woven into major religions, even some Shamanic tradition, though not most, some.

"Let's be clear, there is no He-God. This is an illusion. This is a mythology. Any more than there is a She-God. There is only Source Energy, Light Energy—the Spark; the Divine—the energy that can be expanded through consciousness and exists in a formless state.

"What you think is a long time, isn't. The world is shifting out of its imbalance to a return to wholeness. So, the Divine Feminine has to return. The world has to balance with the recognition of the Divine Feminine."

Eve then said to me, "You want to write about this. But most history is written from the male energy perspective. So much is missing. It's half a story. There is something to be written about that; that so little is told relative to what actually occurred: the rise of the church and temples which happened in relative proximity. It happened all over, in varying regions... like an infection all over."

Patriarchy: How the Hell Did It Happen?

Beginning around 2300 BCE, waves of invaders from the north rode in on horse-drawn chariots, wielding weapons of war and the determination to conquer the peaceful, mother-centered lands. These invaders are referred to as "Indo-Europeans." They, unlike others, had perfected the use of the horse-drawn chariot for war. This gave them an advantage that made them essentially unstoppable as an army.

These northern invaders had an entirely different view of society and God. They believed in light vs darkness and good vs evil. (Darkness was believed to be inferior, suggesting racial attitudes towards dark-skinned people.) They believed that a Father God reigned supreme and that His representatives were men. They imposed a caste system and a patriarchy and they held a special contempt for the Mother Goddess. Merlin Stone points out:

> What is most significant to us is that in historic times the northern invaders viewed themselves as a superior people. This attitude seems to have been based upon their ability to conquer the more culturally developed earlier settlers, the people of the Goddess. The Indo-Europeans were in continual conflict not only with the people whose lands they invaded but between themselves as well. The pattern that surfaces in each area in which they made an appearance is that a group of aggressive warriors, accompanied by a priestly caste of high standing, who initially invaded, conquered and then ruled the indigenous people of each land they entered." (*When God Was a Woman*)

The God of the Indo-Europeans was a storm God who ruled from high on a mountaintop and showed himself in a blaze of fire. He held contempt for the female. Now, God was always male, the champion, supreme and the powerful ruler of others.

The people of Crete were pottery-makers, weavers, and artists who developed sophisticated irrigation systems. They were a highly organized, peaceful society of 100,000 people from the year 6000

BCE. Sjöö and Mor write, "We are taught that Western civilization begins with Greece, but in fact the imagination of the Greeks came from Crete. All Greek religious ritual, all Greek mythology, was of Cretan-Mycenaean origin." Crete was the very last flourishing matriarchal culture.

The northern invaders decimated the Cretan way of life and replaced the Cretan democratic social structure with a caste system. In the end, the invasion of the northerners, followed by a catastrophic earthquake, destroyed the last of the Goddess-worshipping cultures by 1400 BCE.

In my reading with Lori, Eve explained how a "virus" contaminated the women-oriented societies of places like Catal Huyuk and Crete. This matched up as a perfect metaphor for the invasion of patriarchal war energy of the Indo-Europeans. Their way of life was toxic. They entered like a virus invades the human body, infecting the people's way of life and sickening their culture.

In her book, *The Chalice and The Blade*, Riane Eisler writes about, "How the original partnership direction of Western culture veered off into a bloody five-thousand-year dominator detour." She further explains, "The title The Chalice and the Blade derives itself from this cataclysmic turning point during which the prehistory of Western civilization, when the direction of our cultural evolution was quite literally turned around... From worship of the life-generating, feminine, mothering powers of the Universe to 'the lethal power of the blade.'"

Eisler, who fled from the Nazis as a child, explains the choice we now have before us to either return to partnership societies that thrive on mutual cooperation, reverence for life and the feminine, or perpetuate dominator models in which we will inevitably all die from a form of violence by the blade. Today, of course, the blade has become the nuclear missile warhead and/or the continued pathological destruction of our environment.

God as a Woman Timeline:

35,000-40,000 years ago: Venus of Hohle Fels was carved in mammoth's tusk.

25,000 years ago: Venus of Willendorf was carved into limestone.

7500 BCE Catal Huyuk is settled

3000 BCE: History begins with the invention of writing

2700-1100 BCE Minoan Greek Civilization

2300 BCE: First invasions of Indo-Europeans

1400 BCE: Final destruction of matriarchal culture in Crete

200 BCE-200 CE: Hebrew Bible is canonized with the story of Eve in the Book of Genesis

500 CE The last Goddess temple is closed.

313 CE Emperor Constantine declares Christianity the religion of Rome.

1692: Salem Witch Trials

1864: First Known Discovery of Divine Mothers

1961: Discovery of "The Seated Woman"

1960s and 1970s: Trailblazing books were published, including *When God Was a Woman* by Merlin Stone; *The Gods and Goddesses of Old Europe* by Marija Gimbutas; *The Myth of the Goddess* by Jules Cashford and Anne Baring; *The Hebrew Goddess* by Raphael Patai; and *The Chalice and the Blade* by Riane Eisler

2008: The most recent discovery of a mythic Mother Venus Figure

Herstory/History Comparison Chart

Herstory	History
Considered by those in power to be illegitimate and made up.	Considered by those in power to be legitimate and real.
Buried	Above ground.
Expressed in figures.	Expressed in letters.
Hidden	Overt
Interpreted by men and women.	Interpreted by men.
Silent	Loud
Old	Young
Requires descending - going down to discovery and access power. One descends into caves and caverns. High value is placed on introspection. Energy flows through the solar plexus.	Requires ascension to feel powerful: The higher, the better. For example, skyscrapers. Values expansiveness.
Values internal power, inner knowing, intuition and connection with the earth.	Values external force, wealth, expansion and dominance over the earth.
Settles disputes through compromise. No army. Inherently collaborative.	Settles disputes through force. Relies on armies. Inherently competitive.
Economically homogenous. People's basic needs for food, shelter and community are met.	Economically stratified. People are very rich or very poor. Some live extravagantly while others die of starvation and exposure.
Sense of belonging.	Feeling of disenfranchisement.
Nonviolent society.	Pervasive violence.
Able to sustain peace over long period of time.	Warring society with intermittent periods of peace.

Spiritual Exercise

Images of The Mother God

"At the very dawn of religion," writes Merlin Stone, "God was a woman. Do you remember?"

Look at the images of our Mother Gods on the following pages. What do you notice? What words would you choose to describe them? How do they make you feel? Write down your thoughts here.

You might try drawing them.

How would you create God in the feminine if you had clay, marble or limestone to work with? What would your figure look like?

The Dreaming Goddess of Malta 3200 BCE. Discovered in an underground temple in Malta.

Tell Halaf Figure circa 6000 BCE. Discovered in Southern Turkey in the early 1900's.

Venus of Hohle Fels. Carved out of mammoth ivory, 35,000-40,000 years old. Discovered in 2008, Germany.

Venus of Willendorf, carved in limestone 30,000 years ago. Discovered in 1908, Austria.

**Venus of Dolni. Made of ceramic 29,000-25,000 years old.
Discovered in 1925, Czech Republic.**

Venus de-Laussel, Painted with red ochre and carved into limestone 25,000 years ago. Discovered in 1911 South-Western France.

Minoan Crete Goddess. Made of ceramic in 1700-1400 BCE. Discovered in a temple in Crete, 1903.

Journaling Space

_____
_____
_____
_____
_____
_____
_____
_____
_____
_____
_____
_____
_____
_____
_____
_____
_____
_____
_____
_____
_____
_____
_____
_____
_____
_____

The Sixth Day

How to Access Great Mother Energy

A detail from The Three Ages of Women, Gustav Klimt, oil on canvas, 1905

"There is a healthier self within each of us, just waiting for encouragement"
~Gloria Steinem

Meet the Great Mothers: An Interfaith Experience

*T*hink about someone who loves you deeply and completely. Bring this person into your heart now. This person may be living or living in spirit. This is someone who loves you *just because you are you.* This is someone who you do not worry about having to impress and someone who you know could never be disappointed in you because their only wish is to love you just as you are. When you are with this person, you feel relaxed, safe and comfortable. This is the most nurturing mother you can imagine, or grandmother, aunt, friend, or the very best teacher you ever had in school, whose classroom felt like a cocoon.

This is the energy of the Great Mother.

Now, bring into your attention someone who you love just because they were born, someone who makes you just light up inside to think about and be with. This might be a child or an adult or an animal. When you are with this being, you feel like you want to protect her/him from pain and help her/him be strong. You feel like giving your love is your purpose for being alive. It is as if you share one heart.

Now it is *you* who is feeling the power of being in the state of Great Mother Love.

When I was a little girl, I had a great aunt named Aunt Bessie. Aunt Bessie used to call me, "her little kitten," because I snuggled by her side whenever I came to visit. All my cousins would go off and play together, but I just wanted to burrow into Aunt Bessie's arms. She was a large woman, with folds and rolls and sagging arms that felt like the softest cushions to rest on. It didn't matter to me what she looked like. It mattered only how I felt when I was with her. She was a Great Mother to me.

Recently, I went to hear Elizabeth Gilbert and Martha Beck. I was one of 600 women and 11 brave men who came to spend the weekend basking in the loving brilliance of these two women. Liz and Martha asked the group to request from the Universe what we really needed at this time in our life. From the back of the room, a woman stepped forward. She looked to be in her forties. She took the microphone, closed her eyes and with an exhale that contained many tears, she said, "I need to rest. I'm exhausted. If I could just have ninety days to rest, I think I could heal myself." She began to cry.

I knew how she felt. I knew that level of physical and psychic exhaustion when you can barely carry the weight of your body anymore and you just need time to catch your breath, to rest, restore and be held in the arms of the Great Mother. When you are absolutely used up and you have no more energy but still so much needs to be done; when you sink into self-doubt and hurt, you need the Great Mother.

In her gorgeous book, *The Book of She*, Sara Avant Stover writes about her encounter with Mary Magdalene who came to her one night with a very specific message. "'Sara, my love,' she whispered, lips close to my ear, 'I am here for you now, and always. You have nothing to worry about. You are my daughter. You are here to do my work in the world. Because of this, I will always take care of you. I will never be far away. I am always here with you.' … And in the morning, although Mary Magdalene was physically gone, I still felt Her presence in my depths."

Great Mother Energy can flow from actual people in your life, as with my Aunt Bessie. It can come to you from your loved ones who live in spirit. But it can also come to you from archetypal energies, as in the way that Eve came to me—a loving and powerful force compelling me forward in my life, dislodging me from the chaos I was in and asking me to be exceedingly brave and follow my truth.

As you bring Great Mother Energy into your life, here are two guiding principles:

#1. *You Are Always Welcome*

I never knocked on my grandmother's door. A second after I rang the outside bell of her apartment building, she waited for me with her door wide open and the warmest, "Hi, Tam!" My grandmother was always so excited to see me. She was always available to talk and she was always available to listen. *This is the grandmother's way.*

The same is true when we visit with our Great Mothers. They are always happy to see us. If we "ring the bell" and signal to them that we are coming, they will open their doors and greet us with excitement and love. We never have to knock, for the doors of the Great Mothers are always open to us.

You can visit the Great Mothers at any time. They can be from your own tradition or from other traditions. There are so many Great Mothers for you to draw upon, each with unique qualities. Think of them as energetic systems that are available to you beyond the limitations of any one faith. The Great Mothers are all our mothers. They are all here for you to tap into and allow their power to flow through you. Open yourself to feeling them and how their energy shows itself in you.

Sometimes the Great Mothers are referred to as Goddesses, other times as Divine mothers like Mother Mary, and sometimes they are named for a Divine quality like *Shekinah*, which is the Hebrew word for *presence*. They have different personalities and different ways of reaching you, but they all carry feminine truth, power and light.

Great Mother energy belongs to all of us. It extends to us beyond the boundaries of our own religious upbringings or culture. You do not have to be Catholic to feel the power of Mary. You do not have to be Jewish to let the light of the Feminine Divine flow through you as you light Shabbos candles. You can live in Canada and call in the power of Shakti, the Hindu Goddess of imminent creative expression. Pachamama is not just for Latin Americans. Her power is for anyone who needs the Great Mother to help with abundance and self-sufficiency. You do not betray your own religion by opening yourself to love everywhere. You honor it.

Though it may seem strange at first to journey to meet an Indian Goddess if you have never even been to India, remember that you are a soul in a body. The soul lives in you beyond time and space. It is your soul that connects you to the energy of the Great Mothers and the soul knows no bounds, only love. Sara Avant Stover writes:

> Who is She? Some call her Sophia. Others call her Kuan Yin, Mary, Pachamama, Buffalo Woman, Grandmother Spider,

Isis, Shakti, the Mother. She's the sparkle in your eyes, the wind weaving through the trees, the leap of your dog through the hills outside. She's the very breath you are breathing right now…We all have to find Her, and in finding Her, must learn how and what to call Her. I call her She.

You will discover many names for Great Mother energy. They all carry the energy of the Feminine Divine. This light is available to anyone from any faith or background who seeks to bring it into her life.

The Great Mothers from every different faith and every different place belong to all of us and we, from every faith and every place, belong to them. They are our mothers and we are their daughters.

#2. You Are Her Favorite

I remember when I was a child, sitting with my mother and her three siblings while my grandmother opened her Mother's Day cards. All the family gathered around her with a joy that vibrated through my body. There was so much love for my grandmother, so much respect. There was also a lot of humor.

"Read mine out loud, Mom," my Uncle Carl would call out.

My grandmother shined with love as she opened the card and read the Hallmark poem which was always followed by, "Don't worry, I won't tell the other ones that you said I am your favorite. Love, Your Favorite Son Carl."

With that my grandmother blushed and said, "I didn't say that! You are all my favorites!"

Then Carl's brother would call out, "Mom, open my card next!"

My grandmother then gracefully opened the next card which

would have another lovely Hallmark poem followed by, "Thank you for telling me that I am your favorite. I promise not to tell the others."

"Norman!" My grandmother laughed and laughed and said, "You are all my favorite. I didn't say that!" This teasing continued until my grandmother opened all the cards from all four of her children, all claiming that she told them in secret that they were her favorite. This went on year after year after year.

When my grandmother died, we all gathered to decide what to write on her headstone. The words seemed so very important to hold the space for such a spectacular human being, one whom we loved with all our hearts and soul. What could we write to pay homage to our family's most loving, good-humored, matriarch? My mother suggested, and we all agreed, that at the bottom of her headstone underneath the Hebrew date for her birth and death, it should say, "She made us all her favorite." And so, it was written.

The love from the Great Mothers is infinite but you will feel so very special, like you are Her favorite!

Spiritual Exercise

Visiting with the Great Mothers

Here are some of the many, many names of Great Mothers who you can visit and develop a relationship with. A Great Mother might come to you in a dream, day or night. You may feel that she has something to ask of you, as I did when Eve compelled me to write this book. You may also go to them for wisdom, for healing and for strength. Visit each one as if you are visiting with your own grandmother. Sit with her. Talk with her. Listen to her stories and tell her your own.

> As you visit with each one of them, ask yourself: *Who is this Great Mother? If we were sitting together in the same room, what would I want to talk to her about?*

Pachamama: *World Mother and Mother Earth.* She is revered by the indigenous people of the Andes.

Pachamama is the energy of ripening, nourishment, abundance, fertility and wealth. You can go to Pachamama to give thanks for abundance. You can burn incense to thank Her for the harvests in your life. In the Andes, on the night before August 1ˢᵗ, families stay up all night cooking to celebrate Pachamama and before anyone is allowed to eat, a plate is given to Her. You can ask Pachamama to guide you in experiencing abundance.

Her Truth: *You already have what you need. In fact, you have more than you need. You'll feel this as you give to others, as you share what you have "cooked all night." There is no need to worry. Return to a bountiful state; there is, and always will be, plenty.*

Shekhinah: She comes to us from Jewish tradition. In Hebrew, her name means *presence*; She dwells in us and around us.

The Shekhinah is the Divine Feminine energy that comes to us on Shabbat as a radiant bride. In Kabbalah, Shekinah is the energy of the Feminine Divine that sustains the world. Her light is felt by the light of the moon, reflecting Divinity into the world. You can wrap yourself in the light of the Shekinah for Divine illumination and clarity. She is clear consciousness. On Friday evening when the moon comes up, you can connect to her as you light two candles to welcome the Shabbat.

Her Truth: You *are meant to live in Shalom, or peace. Peace is your natural state. Return to peace.*

Shakti: She comes to us from Hinduism; Her name in Sanskrit means *Creative Energy.*

Shakti is power, strength, capable energy and dynamic force. Shakti energy is the kundalini rising through you from the base of your spine upwards like two coiled snakes. Shakti energy is the creative magic to manifest that which is inside you and longing to be born. Call on her when you need power that is raw, potent, vigorous and compelling.

Her Truth: *You have the power to make your life happen. You have the power to manifest your dreams. You are meant to live in a powerful state of ever-manifesting. You have the power you need. You are <u>much</u> more powerful than you imagine yourself to be!*

Sophia: Her name means wisdom in Greek; in Hebrew She is known as *Chochma,* which also means *wisdom.*

You can connect to Sophia through the wisdom literature in the biblical books of Proverbs, Ecclesiastes and The Book of Solomon. Sophia is the energy that King Solomon drew on to solve the major problems in the land and maintain peace. Sophia is wise, loving counsel. You can draw from her energy to quiet your ego mind and achieve a state of clear knowing. She will help you stay on course, solve conflict and return to a stable, loving way of being.

Her Truth: *You have the ability to solve any problem that you face through generosity, creativity and perspective. There is no problem that you cannot solve. If the problem exists, so does the solution.*

Kuan Yin: *Mother of Compassion.* She comes to us from China, Japan, Malaysia and Burma. She comes to us from Buddhist tradition.

Kuan Yin is imagined as a woman with a thousand arms so as to always be available and able to reach out to you in your suffering. She is imagined as having an eye in the palms of each of Her thousand hands so that she can see you in your suffering. Kuan Yin hears your prayers. She is the great healer. She is tender. You can tell her all about what hurts and she will not judge you. It is said that her voice can be heard in the sound of water running through streams and her presence experienced in jade, the lotus, black tea and rainbows.

Her Truth: *You feel alone. But you are not alone. She is with you. Make space in your loneliness for Her. Sense her. Allow Her to reach you.*

Mother Earth: She is *Mother of Earth*, the heart of many Native traditions.

Mother Earth is alive. She is able to feel. Mother Earth is a sentient being and she is hurting because we have forgotten that nature is sacred. Go to Her with your energy to offer deep gratitude and reverence. Touch the ground. Thank the trees. Feel Her spirit in everything that is alive around you. Go outside and walk by the light of the moon. Be awed by the majesty of it all. She is the most magnificent source of beauty. But don't stop there. The most potent way to connect with Mother Earth at this time is to fight for Her. Fight for Her in whom you elect. Fight for Her by protecting the water and the air around you. As you fight against all forms of poisoning the environment, the spirit of Mother Earth will come to you.

Her Truth: *You are needed at this time to fight for Her life because at this time in the evolution of our species, fighting for Her life is the same as fighting for yourself.*

Into the Divine Sisterhood

Imagine living in a world in which women joined together as Great Mothers! Imagine if Eve knew with absolute certainty that, while she was *stepping out* of the Garden, she was *stepping into* a sisterhood of humanity in which she would never be left alone to suffer—in which the world was continuously getting better and better. How different might that have been for her? Imagine if *you* knew that there were many women supporting you, nurturing you and helping you back up from your knees to stand tall in your life, *how much better would life be for you?*

I grew up listening to my mother talk on the telephone. I would poke her and pull the coils in the cord to get her to hang up, but she talked and talked and talked. (I assure you that she was not neglecting me but at one point I distinctly remember her asking, "What do you think this is that I am holding? Does this look like a tumor attached to my head?")

The telephone calls *were* very important. Susan was getting divorced and Barbara was thinking about getting a divorce. There was a lot of divorce. There was a lot of reassessing. Here were women trying to sort out their marriages and themselves. It was messy and complicated and often very sad. But it was also exciting and inspiring and empowering. They wondered: *Could we do it on our own? Could we make money instead of dinner? Do business instead of laundry? Was it possible to feel good about ourselves? Was it possible to meet our own needs? Were we even allowed to have needs?*

The conversations between my mother and her friends from our kitchen phone in the late 70s made independence sound like candy. Or oxygen. They were coming into their own. They smoked cigarettes, got jobs and bought themselves cars. They counseled each other, cried together, and searched for self-worth together.

They grew strong together. They came to believe in themselves together. They came through for each other. Together. They couldn't have done it without each other. There is no way that individually they would have had the courage to leap off that patriarchal cliff from one way of living to another. The collective strength they garnered was exponentially powerful. They knew that when one leapt, the others were down below holding the net.

"I wrote about you in my book today," I tell my mom.

"Oh- boy! What did you say?"

"I wrote about how you spent my entire childhood talking to Susan in your bathrobe from the kitchen phone. Do you remember when I would interrupt you and you would ask me if I thought the telephone was a tumor growing out of your head?"

"I'm sorry I said that," my Mom replied, "It wasn't very nice." She paused. "But Tam, the telephone wasn't just a telephone. It was my lifeline."

I remember when I was just beginning my career as a young rabbi and made one fatal assumption: I assumed that women would be supportive of me. At least, I naively thought, they would be fair and kind. I never saw it coming.

I'm not saying that men did not give me a hard time. While moving up the temple ranks, I went to battle many times with all kinds of men, young and old, rich and poor, sane and insane. One wanted my job, another wanted me to take a large salary cut. There were men who didn't believe I should be or could be Rabbi Wine's successor. I strapped on my gladiator boots and slew them like the fire-breathing dragons they were. I expected the fight. They were men! *Of course* they were going to have issues with a woman in a position of power. *Of course* they weren't going to know how to deal with boobs on the *bima*. (Hebrew for stage.) It was natural. It was simple too: I would help them evolve or I would kick their asses.

But the women? There was something extra bloody about doing

battle with another woman. It was a tragic loss of opportunity to work together towards a shared vision. It felt like a violation of a sacred agreement.

I dream of a world in which women embolden and emblazon one another instead of competing like men to kill each other off. I dream of a world in which women turn to each other for help, or offer it. I imagine a global sisterhood network of womankind because every woman's success is my success.

There is nothing in the world more powerful than a group of women working together to achieve a common goal.

The power of women in collaboration remains largely untapped and unknown. Though extraordinary achievements have been made, we have never tested what we might be able to do if we had the numbers and confidence of men in places of power and influence. What would the Catholic church be like with women priests? How would the governments be different with women driving policy? I'm not suggesting a complete takeover. I'm just asking us, as women, to begin to imagine such a world.

The Divine Sisterhood will lead the way.

I felt called to "gather the women together" and sent an Evite out before I lost my nerve. I had led hundreds of ceremonies and services but never in my home and never for the purpose of calling in the Feminine Divine. Nearly all the women whom I invited immediately responded "yes." They were eager to be together and to share a purposeful, deep encounter with each other. Intrinsically, everyone seemed to understand what I meant when I invited them into the sacred circle of women and there was an equal understanding of what feminine spirituality felt like.

That night, thirty women sat in a wide circle. On a low table in the middle, I placed candles, river rocks and yellow flowers, creating a kind of altar. The central figure was a large ceramic woman with wide hips and an elongated neck sitting in the lotus position with her second finger and thumb touching to signal meditation. Where, you might ask, did I find this perfect sacred piece of art? At Costco. She appeared on the left in the garden section. *Perfect!* I think I said out loud and swiftly put her in my cart. *She will represent the Goddess!*

I lit a candle and placed it in the concave of her lap. The fire brought her to life and she was the center piece at my first gathering.

The women ranged in age from my eleven-year-old daughter, who floated in and out of the room per the whims of her attention span, to several women in their mid-seventies. Our religious backgrounds varied greatly but had no bearing. I sat next to my friend who wore a Hijab. This is an important quality of feminine spirituality: inclusivity of all religious differences, age differences and even gender differences. In a woman's circle, the exclusivity of male-dominated religion is replaced by the high value placed on inclusivity and celebration of diversity. We were spiritual women there to engage the Divine Feminine and whatever made us different made us even more beautiful.

We began by listening to the song "I'm Ready" by Tracy Chapman. We felt a deep sense of relief, pleasure, emotional vulnerability and even love, as we tuned into ourselves in the presence of soul sisters. There was a full sense of "spirit" in the act of just sitting together and allowing our hearts to feel what they feel. So many of us had spent so much of our lives trying to get out of our hearts and into our heads. It was so completely delicious to just sit quietly and listen to the whispers within.

"In every moment the universe is whispering to you. There are messages for you carried on the winds. There is wisdom for you in the morning songs of the birds outside your window and in the soft murmurs of an ebbing sea. Even ordinary, everyday events in your life carry communications from the realm of spirit..."
~Denise Linn

Some of the women closed their eyes, some cried, some smiled. All emotions and all responses were equally welcome. This is very much the nature of feminine spirituality: allowing emotion to emerge organically without agenda or judgment. It was key to sit in a circle, as the circle represents the fluidity of life, the strength of connections and the absence of hierarchal power structure. In the circle, I was not the leader. I was a facilitator. Ah, what a relief!

After we listened to the song I asked the question: *What are you ready for?* The women answered by saying:

"I'm ready for a new spirituality."

"I'm ready to love myself."

"I'm ready to connect with other women."

"I'm ready to come out of hiding."

"I'm ready for a woman-made God."

What are *you* ready for?

When women sit together in a circle and let in the light together, Eve smiles. She is healing us and we are healing her. Try listening to Tracy Chapman's song and see what it brings to you. Maybe you will discover what YOU are ready for!

It is the journey of every woman to find the voice of Eve that was lost that first day. Now, after generations and generations of girls and women living in oppression, *we* have enough collective courage to ungag ourselves.

We are taking off our fig leaves and standing naked before God!

We are out of hiding. We were born; therefore, we are Divinely lovable. Love is our birthright. In this state of personal power, we are ready to reclaim the Feminine Divine. We are ready to reclaim the truth about ourselves too. Anything that is not kind or not loving is not ours. A great burden is being lifted from our shoulders and we now stand tall, ready for the next journey. I wonder what is up ahead? The future is wide and open. What are YOU ready for? As women, we have just begun to reinvent the world.

We were returning to the circle and to a flow of life between women who gather together to tell their stories and heal each other. Bone by bone, we were remembering who we once were, how women had lived before patriarchy going all the way back to the Paleolithic era some 35,000 years ago. We were remembering how we were meant to treat each other as sacred, Divine sisters. **We were becoming Great Mothers to ourselves and to each other.**

Going Back with Great Mother Love

After Eve, many things happen in the Bible, many events unfold. Generations come and go, cities are destroyed and new ones are built, an entire people leave one land and journeys to another, but no one, not a single person—not even God—goes back for Eve. Eve is abandoned in the beginning of history.

"Mmm…" Now I'm thinking.

Can this be changed? Can what was taken from her be retrieved?

What if *we* could help her?

What if *we* could go back and get her?

What if we could actually retrieve Eve and all her Divine light?

Could a critical mass of women energetically bring Eve out of banishment and into the sacred community of women, to greet her, soothe her and restore her rightful place in the order of the Universe? Could we, the women alive today, journey thousands of years into the past as Great Mothers, retrieve Eve and restore her to her rightful place as our spiritual Mother? Could we recover the lost light of Eve by going back to her as wounded healers?

I have a friend who grew up in an abusive home. No one rescued her. No one came to help. "When I was seven years old," she told me, "it occurred to me—God had forgotten me." This thought, she said, was even more devastating than the abuse because it left her feeling utterly bereft and abandoned.

Imagine what it could mean to Eve if <u>we</u> didn't forget her, what it mean to her if we went back for her. Can you imagine how good that would feel, if, on an energetic level, hundreds, thousands, millions of women came streaming over the desert hills with their arms open, some singing, others gently calling her name and still others, silent. We would be a recognizable sea of healing, a stream of life coming to the Mother herself; a Haj, a sacred pilgrimage to Jerusalem, an act of atonement and redemption. This would be the largest interfaith gathering for Eve and all women who were persecuted for being women, since history began.

Eve deserves an act of love on that scale, and so do you.

You can heal yourself by going back for yourself. This, I believe, is one of the most healing, beautiful acts of love that you will ever do for yourself. Think about all the times when you felt desperately alone or ashamed or very, very frightened, especially when you were a little girl. You can energetically go back in time with love and heal yourself.

I imagine doing this for Eve.

We find Eve out in the middle of a field, utterly alone and in a state of physical and emotional collapse. She's looks broken—like she has literally been dropped from several stories up. She's "Fallen." Several of her ribs are broken and she is in indescribable pain.

"Where does it hurt?" We ask, almost frantic.

"Everywhere," Eve tell us and begins to weep. We stabilize her body, but she is inconsolable.

She just keeps repeating, "I hurt. I hurt." And she won't show us her face.

Eve is more than hurt. She is humiliated.

When we meet her, she looks like the most incredible pool of radiant golden light with a puncture wound in the center. Her life force energy is leaking through a hole in her energy field.

We can literally see it—how she is losing Grace.

The first person to reach Eve wraps her in her arms. Then another woman comes and holds her too. From there, we take each other's hands and hold each other and walk together and dance and sit together in silence. We realize that what we need the most is just to be present to each other's experiences. We just need time to be with each other and to embrace each other just as we each are in the moment. Most of the women, including Eve, are exhausted and need deep rest. Someone begins making soup. Someone else begins singing. Others just sit together. We initiate the ancient art of regenerating each other.

Later that night, we begin to tell our stories. We tell Eve the same thing that we each need to know: *You didn't do anything wrong. I am here with you. You can do it. I will be right by your side as long as you need me.*

Becoming Your Own Great Mother

Our inner child carries most of the shame that we bear our entire lives. It's like picking a heavy suitcase up off the baggage claim and schlepping it with you for the next eighty years! What's more – it's not even your suitcase!

But it doesn't have to be that way. You can heal from shame quite well and since it is the most painful spiritual wound, the sooner the better.

Here is how: *Tend to the life of your inner child.*

We all have an inner child living in us. Our inner child carries all the memories and emotions of what happened to us as we grew up. And, often unbeknownst to us, that inner child often drives our emotions and behavior as adults. The parts of our inner child that are injured need and deserve our loving attention. And this is how it works: The more you lovingly get to know the child that lives in you, the more relief you will feel.

At first, paying attention to your inner child may seem silly or awkward, but with practice it will feel very natural. Please don't judge this. Your mind will take you off track. Go to your inner child with your heart and soul, not with your mind.

We heal as we come for our inner child. We hold her. We soothe her. We love her unconditionally. You can rock her to sleep in your own arms or take her for ice cream.

Spiritual Exercise

The Front Steps

Imagine that you see your inner child sitting outside by herself on the steps of your childhood home. Notice what she is wearing. Notice how she seems to be feeling. Notice what she is doing. Is she still or playing? Is she loud or quiet?

Now, gently and quietly, sit down on the steps next to her, say hello, and spend a few moments talking with her. You might share that you are her adult self, and that you are here to listen to her and help her feel good in the world. When you are both ready, try getting to know your inner child by asking her some questions:

- What makes you feel good?
- How do you find rest?
- What do you like to do during the day just for fun?
- What frightens you?
- What do you worry about? How long have you been worried about that?
- How can I help you feel safe?

Consider that she might have some questions for you. Allow yourself to go back to those front steps anytime to get to know her better.

Spiritual Exercise

Beautiful Baby

Imagine yourself as a baby. See your baby self in your own arms. Sweet, new to the earth, a miracle of life. Now ask yourself: Does this baby have to earn love? Is this baby capable of being bad? Is it even possible that this baby, who is your baby self, deserves any form of rejection? As you hold your baby self in your arms, send this lullaby deep into your being: *I was born, therefore, I am lovable. I was born; therefore, I am lovable.* Hold your baby self and let the light of the Divine shine down upon you. Love that baby like the miracle she is and your link to Heaven on Earth.

Loving all children, especially the inner child that lives inside all of us, is the way to Paradise.

The more love, compassion and "Great-Mothering" you give to yourself, the more you will be able to experience with other people.

Spiritual Exercise

Becoming a Love Conductor

> Read this meditation through once or twice, then you will be able to remember how to do it and you can close your eyes to begin your practice.

Find a position that is comfortable for you. Take a few deep, slow breaths. When you are ready, close your eyes. Continue to breathe naturally and easily. Now place one of your hands on your heart, gently touching the center of your beating lifeforce. You're tuning into your heart now. Take a few breaths, then gently place your other hand on your face, along your cheek, the way someone who adores you would place their hand on you. Hold yourself in this way for a few breaths with love and reverence for who you are, the way someone who adores you would behold you. Notice how it feels to behold yourself this way.

Bringing your attention now to your heart, become aware of all those you love. They can be living in the world or living in spirit. They can be people or animals. One by one, let the names of your loved ones come to you. Feel your love going from your heart to them. The love might look like water; it might look like light. It might have a color or many colors. It might even be sound. All this love is pouring forth from your heart, through your hand and into the Universe to the beings you love.

Now bring your attention to your other hand that is resting on your face. Begin to feel the love of everyone who loves you. Living or living in spirit. Feel the love of every person, every animal, who loves you. <u>Remembering that love doesn't die.</u> All the love that you ever experienced is right here available to you. Call that energy into you through your hand. One by one, name by name. You are receiving love from all the beings who love you. See this energy come in through your hand, saturating your face. Feel the light flowing down the back of your throat and down into your heart center. Perhaps the energy has a color or many colors. Maybe it has a temperature or a consistency, like water or air. All this love is coming to you through your hand, into your face and head, down your throat and into your heart.

You are now conducting a great love orchestra with both hands. With one you receive and with the other, you give. You might even allow your hands to begin to dance in the air around your head and your heart—playing with the music of light as it flows in and out and all around you. Send the love into your torso, your legs and arms. Send out the love from your torso, your legs and your arms. Imagine there is so much love all around you that you can no longer distinguish what is going out and what is coming in. Lavender light, golden light, blue light, merge into white light. "This is how I shall live," you say. "I shall live in Grace."

After you open your eyes say this out loud again three times: *This is how I shall live. I shall live in Grace.* Give yourself a big hug, holding yourself in your own arms for a few gentle, quiet moments. Take a deep cleansing breath, placing your hands in prayer pose and gently pushing them together; seal your practice. *Namaste. Shalom. Amen.*

161

Journaling Space

_____
_____
_____
_____
_____
_____
_____
_____
_____
_____
_____
_____
_____
_____
_____
_____
_____
_____
_____
_____
_____
_____
_____
_____
_____
_____

The Seventh Day

Life as a Free Bird

She Flourishes, oil on canvas, Gaia Orion, 2019 gaiaorion.com

"What will be the collective accomplishments that women of our times will leave on our culture, our values, our families, our country, and our aching planet? The human family is waiting. Hoping. Leadership is not for everyone but if you have heard its call, I urge you to answer. What are you waiting for? Dare to lead."
~Anne Doyle, Powering Up! How America's Women Achievers Become Leaders

The Spiritual Imperative of Our Time

*W*hen he was in high school, my son Lior, to my delight, became a feminist. We had this conversation:

"Imagine that Dad was the only parent's voice that you ever heard," I explain to him, "Imagine that everything you know, you learned from him. I am completely silent. I'm here but I cannot speak or teach or even gesture. And after I die there will be no stories about me, and after a generation no one will remember anything I said. I will have no lasting influence. Everything you will ever know will be filtered through Dad's perceptions. How different would you be?"

"That wouldn't be good." Lior breaks out a big funny smile like *eek*, then adds, "I'd be really off!"

"You'd be off balance?" I ask him.

"*Really* off balance." Lior chuckles.

We—the world—are really off balance. The Feminine Divine is returning to us at this time because we are in desperate need of Her to rebalance us. In fact, it is now or never.

We live in an ironic world. Never have we been able to produce more food and feed more people, yet we live in a world filled with poverty and starvation. We figured out how to walk on the moon and visit Mars, but we have not stopped human trafficking. Never have women been freer, more powerful and more equal, yet never have they been more marginalized and oppressed. It has never been a better time to be born a girl, but it has also never been worse. We are living in a world in which some women lead corporations and countries, while others spend most of the day walking miles for fresh water, risking rape and death, just to get a drink. We can communicate in an instant to anyone anywhere, yet we still do not know how to make peace with each other. Most urgently, the planet can no longer regenerate itself from the garbage we dump. As a person alive today, I cannot say for certain that by the time my great-grandchildren are born, there will be enough clean air to breathe or clean water to swim, anywhere on planet Earth.

"The pollution of the planet is only an outward reflection of an inner psychic pollution: millions of unconscious individuals not taking responsibility for their inner space."
~Eckhart Tolle

In 2009, the Dalai Lama astonished an audience in Vancouver by announcing, "The world will be saved by Western women." What did he mean? Surely, he didn't mean that Western women were any better than any other women on the planet. And what about men? Can't they save the world?

He was giving Western women their mission, their Divine purpose to unite and act according to the ethical imperatives of the sacred feminine. He was empowering us to step up as a collective and use our unprecedented power and access to resources to become a force for healing the likes of which the world has never seen. His words were both a plea and an endorsement. He was asking us to wake up to our purpose for being alive on the planet today.

Women have just begun to invent the world. Our talents, our perspectives, our experiences, have just begun to be integrated into politics, business, medicine and spirituality. Imagine a world in which the feminine perspective has had time to work its way into how we relate to God, our bodies, our businesses and our government? What might a world in which women leadership reaches a tipping point look like? How much better might our chances be for solving the chronic maladies of our time like violence, hunger, pollution and planetary suffering?

If we, as women, truly joined together for who we really are: beings of Divine God-Light refracted through our soul and living in our 37.2 trillion cells—how different could we make our home here, outside of Eden? If Eve had known with absolute certainty that while she was *stepping out* of the Garden, she was *stepping into* a sisterhood of humanity in which she would never be left alone to suffer, how different might it have been for her? If *you* knew that there were many women supporting you, nurturing you and helping you back up from your knees to stand tall in your life, how much better would life be for you? Imagine how much better it *can be*, together, and with Eve's guidance. She is returning to help us save ourselves.

We are being asked to do nothing short of birth a new consciousness for our species.

In increasing numbers people are dissatisfied with the patterns of force, dominance, and external power that have defined us over the last 2,000 years. Imperialism, colonialism, and materialism have lost their allure. In the West, with all our "stuff," we feel increasingly empty. We are longing for interconnectedness. We are longing for deep relationships. We want simple peace without and within.

Many people alive on the planet today have outgrown old structures of masculine power. We no longer trust our governments. We question all authority.

And most importantly, we see many of the old "truths" about God, man and the place of women for what they really are: lies.

We are ready to shed all the self-doubt and all the shame that ever held us back. We are dying to be reborn. Anne Baring says it this way:

> The feminine asks that war and the creation of weapons of destruction are relinquished, just as racism and conquests in the name of God or any other ideology need to be relinquished... In recognizing her depression, her suffering, her longing to outgrow the subservience and powerlessness of her past and present experience, in recognizing and supporting her deepest values, she may accomplish some-

thing truly heroic and extraordinary for life and the planet, something that humanity in centuries to come will celebrate. For this reason, nothing is of such importance as woman's rescue of herself.

The Feminine Divine is returning to us now for a reason, a sacred purpose. **She is here to restore balance.** Western women will save the world. We have our marching orders.

There is a direct correlation between what was done to the Mother God and what is currently being done to Mother Earth. Both were stripped of their sacredness. Both were defiled. Patriarchy took the Supreme Mother and mercilessly reduced her in size until she was so small that she fit like a broken genie stuffed back into a bottle. That bottle was then dropped into a deep hole in the earth, sinking ever deeper by the generations who knew neither her name nor the Divine treasure buried beneath their very feet. Only Eve remained to tell her story, a distorted cruel version of the first exquisite, most perfect truth: **We are *all* created in the Divine's image.** A woman's silence and shame became the haunting vestiges of Her once glorious, most loving existence. And the spiritual imperative of our time: *How to reject and correct this damning inheritance?*

Spiritual Exercise

A New Myth of Eve

Now that you have awakened to the myth of Eve and discovered who Eve really is and who she can be, *how would you retell her story? You* have a message and it is time for it to be known. How would you write a new myth of Eve? Now you have the power to bring the light of the Feminine Divine to shine upon us!

A New Myth of Eve:

_____

_____

_____

_____

_____

_____

_____

_____

_____

_____

_____

_____

_____

_____

_____

_____

On the Seventh Day...

On the Seventh Day, God looked around and saw the glory of the sky and the majesty of the mountains and how the dream She dreamed of creating the cosmos had become the cosmos. She yearned to share what She knew with women. She recognized this yearning as love, to impart on another all that is good in oneself. So, she inhaled the deepest, most awesome inhale, compelling all the oxygen on planet Earth to Her and then... exhaled into the hearts of women everywhere, and by then there were billions.

We felt it—Her breath going into our lungs. It was an incredible experience of inner expansion, as if all of a sudden we could finally breathe. It felt as if all of a sudden we were stronger and could think clearly. Then came the most delicious feeling of empowerment, as if we could actually do whatever it was we were aching to do and become whoever it was we were aching to become, which was almost always just to know the depths of who we already were.

We were experiencing agency—the capacity to create for ourselves. All over the planet, women began creating—weavers wove all night long on luminous looms, their fingers dancing effortlessly and tirelessly with threads as light as music notes. Businesswomen transacted transactions that opened and closed as easily as a hand and brought to the land abundance and harmony. Mothers, daughters, sisters, all created. We birthed children. We birthed communities.

No woman doubted her ability or her right to create. No woman doubted herself. All women lived in relationship to their creative desire... We planted and we reaped in a creative cycle of ever-coming-into-being.

And it was good. So very, very good.

Spiritual Exercise

Your Turn to Write a New Story of Creation

It is now your turn to dream up how you want the world to be. Have chutzpah! Give yourself permission to embody the voice of God and create the world just as you want it to be. You might focus just on your life. You might focus on your city, country, take a global point of view or even speak as Mother Nature. Imagine that you have the power of God; use it to write a new Creation!

On the Seventh Day...

_____

_____

_____

_____

_____

_____

_____

_____

_____

_____

_____

_____

And She saw that it was good. Very, very good.

Today

"You're going to regret this," the temple board member hissed, slithering like a snake around the back of my chair.

Her words sent chills down the nape of my neck like ice chips. I was terrified. *What if she was right? What if I never got another job as a rabbi, never earned enough money or shared my message with anybody, anywhere again?* And worse, what if I woke up the next morning and realized that I'd made a terrible, terrible mistake and felt that certain kind of nausea I remember feeling as a desperately homesick kid stuck all summer at sleepaway camp? No matter how hard I begged and pleaded, my parents would not come pick me up. Right or wrong, they thought sticking it out would make me stronger.

Is it going to be like that? Would I feel hollow inside and ache like that? Because no one was coming to pick me up that day either, not from that board meeting.

I fell. Hard. And I didn't fall gracefully. I did not glide down through the clouds like a ballerina or a princess. The way I fell was embarrassingly messy and excruciatingly public. When I fell, my guts spilled out all over the pavement.

I was down on the ground, just like Eve, draped over, naked, exposed, and so ashamed with a discarded poisonous apple by my side. One bite missing.

How the hell am I going to get up? I thought to myself. I knew I had to. I knew my young children were watching me and that I had to show them that the Universe can kick your ass but you don't stay down on the ground forever. I had to show them that. I was their mother, for God's sake! But here's the thing… I really, really did not know how.

This book, the one that you are holding in your hands right now, is my how. This is the story of how I got up. This is my exit story.

I exited Humanistic Judaism and entered a spirituality that matched my inner truth. One that included the eternity of the soul, Divine energy, and feminine light. One that included my beloved

Eve not just as a biblical story but as a living energy field and a consciousness that has the potential to heal the world. I needed something as big as that to fly with.

I found my wings.

As I look back now, I fully realize that I couldn't have done it any other way. There was no way that I would have been able to leave a place that I loved so much, a place whose bones were my bones without a catapulting, crisis event. I wouldn't say that I'm grateful for it, exactly, but I deeply understand why it had to be as it had to be.

I wish I could tell you that I'm over it all now. But the truth is, seven years later, I still dream about the temple. In my dream, I'm always "after the Fall" and trying to find a way out one of the doors of the temple before anyone sees me inside the building. But I can't get out fast enough. Sometimes in the dream I'm actually naked and there's nowhere to hide. I just HAVE to get out of there! Once I do, I have an even bigger problem: I can't find my car in the temple parking lot. I keep pushing the fav button on my keys but I can't hear it beep! It's not where I left it. *Where the hell is my car?*

After so many nights of dreaming this dream, I've almost become convinced that if Eve had a car, after the Fall we'd find her lost in the temple parking lot, running around naked, frantically pushing the button on her fav key.

I wish I could end this book by saying, "I completely forgive myself and anyone who caused me harm." I wish I could wrap it all up in a beautiful package like a gift and tie it with the perfect red bow. But that would only be partially true.

"To be human is to be lost in the woods."
~Elizabeth Lesser

I do forgive myself. I do forgive the others. I certainly ask for forgiveness and regret any harm that I caused. But it's forgiveness in progress. It's forgiveness as a verb, not as a noun. Every day, I work at it, centimeter by centimeter. One day I'll (gladly) stop dreaming about the temple. One day I will release the very last bits of shame, anger and fear that I have been carrying inside me all my life. And poof! They will evaporate like steam into thin air. Goddess willing.

Today, I am passionate about women's spirituality and the reemergence of the Feminine Divine—how She moves through us and what She is asking of us today as Divine sisters. I believe with my whole heart and soul that WE are our best chance to survive and thrive on this gorgeous water home of ours. We are our best chance to make life here habitable and loving. So, it's crystal clear: We have our mission. I'm betting on the women.

Never, ever underestimate the power of women on a mission.

In the Bible, after seven years, a field is laid fallow so it has time to regenerate. Our ancestors knew that seven years marked a complete organic cycle of growth.

Like that field, over the past seven years I have experienced a complete growth cycle. I am at once the same and forever changed. I am still afraid yet brave, sensitive yet strong, wise, yet ever aware of all that I just don't know. No matter how old I get, I find that inside I am still the same me I have been since I was a very, very little girl, with all the same fears and all the same delights. Yet, it is equally true that I have grown so much in the past seven years as to be almost unrecognizable. Now, I can clearly hear my calling: *To help the energy of the Feminine Divine reemerge in order to bring light, truth and powerful healing to people, especially women, and to Mother Earth.*

Now more than ever I honor myself, know how to soothe myself and nurture myself with the brilliant love that flows from the Great

Mother. Now, I trust myself. Implicitly and completely. I no longer doubt what I know I know. Period.

I am now connected to a current of Divine energy that never leaves me. This energy is a constant source of reassurance, love, light and truth that pulses within me like a spiritual heartbeat. It never stops beating. I have learned how to sense this energy coming from other people and even coming from the body of Mother Earth. Feeling this energy, conducting it and sharing it with other people is my spiritual practice. It is real and tangible and it is so, so very exciting!

Today, I work with women and men to heal their lives and discover their power. I hold interfaith sacred ceremonies. I teach people how to access their truth, follow it and, most tenderly, feel the love of the Great Mother. I teach from the viewpoint of the Feminine Divine—Her calling, Her yearning and Her trust in our power to find our way back to Her and to ourselves. I love, absolutely love, feeling the power of women in groups. We have so much to give to one another and to receive.

I never found another temple home, though maybe someday I will.

And what about "the snake" who hissed in my ear? Was she right? Did I regret it? Did I wake up one morning and realize that I made a terrible, terrible mistake?

No. Not by a long shot.

Sure, I regretted not having my salary and health insurance. Most profoundly, I missed my childhood temple home, where throughout my life I had shared some very special moments and some very special relationships. I missed that. But I never regretted leaving. Never. And neither will you.

You will NEVER regret following your truth. You may hurt. You may reel at the world and feel ashamed and scared and lost, maybe even for a very, very long time, but you will NEVER regret it.

It might happen that when you step out onto the field and stand under the brightest spotlights of your life and all you want is for the crowds to roar with applause, they won't. In fact, they might even try to boo you off the field. But if you do not give up—if you follow the voice of Eve compelling <u>you</u> to be <u>you</u>, to fully and unapologetically claim yourself and have the capacity and audacity to follow your truth—you will have gained something far more precious than the approval of others. You will have learned how to listen for the sound of your own applause. You will have learned how to hear the call of the Feminine Divine.

For 2,000 years feminine power has been shut down. No group of people has experienced more oppression and violence than we have. We have been slayed, burned, hung on the gallows, gagged, exploited, raped, mutilated, and silenced.

But the time has come for us to recover from this history and step into our power individually and collectively. *"The day when mountains move has come,"* wrote Japanese feminist poet Yosano Akiko in 1911. *"Though I say this, nobody believes me. Mountains sleep only for a little while that once have been active in flames... All the women who slept, now awaken and move."*

We are awakening. Like mountains, we are moving.

What was the force that I felt during that terrible board meeting, like a strong hand on my back pushing me to move on? What was it that made me feel so absolutely compelled to follow my truth?

That force was the call of the Feminine Divine and that energy that blasted through me, daring me to pick that apple, be exceedingly brave and follow my truth? That, my dear sister, that was Eve.

At this time in the history of our species, we are being asked to step it up and be daring. We are being asked to refute poisonous mythology, love ourselves and come through for each other-daringly.

We are being asked to reimagine God and what a Feminine Divine presence can do to transform the world from one in which we are dying, to one in which we are being reborn.

We will no longer be silent. We will no longer cooperate in our own oppression and we will not oppress each other. We are women on the rise, flying in formation because together we can fly so much higher.

We are done shrinking down from who we truly are and who we yearn to be. We have awakened to the heat pulsing in the center of our hearts like a fire lit by the Phoenix herself. We will no longer resist the urge to spread our wings and test them in the wind.

My name is Rabbi Tamara Kolton and I am here to report a crime.

They lied to us. They told us that Eve was a sinner. Then they told us that we were sinners so we'd better be pretty and pretty silent.

But we don't believe any of their lies anymore. Today we know the truth.

Truth vs Lies: It's Apples to Oranges

"When it's over," writes Mary Oliver, *"I want to be able to say, all my life, I was a bride married to amazement. I was the bridegroom taking the world into my arms."*

We are charged now with the privilege and the responsibility to write new stories: healing, kind, generous stories. This is the call of the Feminine Divine. It's the call of Eve, our Spiritual Mother, who was lost to us millenniums ago. It is a call to all of us to return to our essential, powerful womanhood.

"Don't be satisfied with stories," says Rumi.
"How things have gone with others.
Unfold your own myth."

There is a better way to live. A much, much better way. We do not have to be stuck in a chronic state of war within ourselves and with each other. <u>War is learned behavior.</u> It's time to unlearn it. Peace is our natural state. Peace is our birthright. Peace is our Divine inheritance. There was a time when we lived in peace, when we knew no other way. There was a time when people revered the feminine and women and men shared power equally. There was a time when God was a woman. *Do you remember?*

My beloved sisters, together we are writing new stories— amazing new stories, like this one.

Because far from being a disobedient sinner, Eve is the Mother of Spiritual Bravery.

Eve is a badass.

Eve is so very, very beautiful.

So are you.

Spiritual Exercise

YOU Are the Empowered Storyteller

Stories can trap our power. They can also release it and empower us. What is a "story" you were told or believe about yourself that constricts your power? How can you change the story to retrieve your power and the TRUTH of who you are and how you are meant to live?

Call on the energy of the Feminine Divine to release any and all of your energy that is trapped in a story about you that does not serve your best life. Begin by writing a new story for yourself here. Amaze yourself!

My Empowered Story:

References

Akiko, Yosano. (1997). *River of Stars: Selected poems of Yosano Akiko*. Translated by Sam Hamill and Keiko Matsui Gibson. Shambhala Publications.

Amichai, Y. (2006). Open Closed Open. Mariner Books.

Baring, A., & Cashford, J. (1993). *The Myth of the Goddess: Evolution of an Image*. Penguin UK.

Doyle, A. (2011). *Powering Up: How America's Women Achievers Become Leaders*. Xlibris Corporation.

Eisler, R. (2011). *The Chalice and the Blade: Our History, Our Future*. Harper Collins.

Estés, C. P. (2008). *Women Who Run with the Wolves: Contacting the Power of the Wild Woman*. Random House.

Hindley, Emma (Producer), Hooper, Louise (Director), Foreman, Amanda (Writer/Presenter) & MacGregor, Hugo (Director). (2016). The Ascent of Woman. [Video file]. Retrieved from https://www.amazon.com/dp/B01HFFC8IY

Gimbutas, M. (2001). *The Living Goddesses*. University of California Press.

Heschel, S. (1983). *On Being a Jewish Feminist: A Reader*. Schocken.

Jewish Women's Archive. "Alphabet of Ben Sira 78: Lilith." (Viewed on August 3, 2019) https://jwa.org/media/alphabet-of-ben-sira-78-lilith>.

Kolton, Tamara, PhD. (2018). *The First Story in the Bible was the First Case of #MeToo*. Retrieved from https://forward.com/scribe/393778/the-first-story-in-the-bible-was-the-first-case-of-metoo/

Lesser, E. (2005). *Broken Open: How Difficult Times Can Help Us Grow*. Random House.

Linn, D. (1996) *The Secret Language of Signs: How to Interpret the Coincidences and Symbols in Your Life*. Ballantine Books.

McNelis, K. (2017). *Your Messy Brilliance: 7 Tools for the Perfectly*

Imperfect Woman: Enrealment Press.

Obama, M. (2018) *Becoming*. Viking, an Imprint of Penguin Books.

Oliver, M. (2017). *Devotions: The Selected Poems of Mary Oliver*: Penguin.

Plaskow, J. (1991). *Standing Again at Sinai: Judaism from a Feminist Perspective*. Harper Collins.

Remen, R. N. (2002). *Kitchen Table Wisdom: Stories That Heal*. Pan Australia.

Roth, G. (1992). *When Food is Love: Exploring the Relationship between Eating and Intimacy*. Penguin.

Roth, G. (2011). *Women, Food and God: An Unexpected Path to Almost Everything*. Simon and Schuster.

Steinem, G. (1993). *Revolution from Within: A Book of Self-Esteem*. Little, Brown and Company.

Stover, S. A. (2015). *The Book of She: Your Heroine's Journey into the Heart of Feminine Power*. New World Library.

Sjöö, M., & Mor, B. (2013). *The Great Cosmic Mother: Rediscovering the Religion of the Earth*. Harper Collins.

Stone, M. (2012). *When God Was a Woman*. Doubleday.

Ted Talk of Burke, Tarana. https://blog.ted.com/propelled-by-possibility-tarana-burke-speaks-at-tedwomen-2018/

Ted Talk of Ziauddin Yousafzai. https://www.ted.com/talks/ziauddin_yousafzai_my_daughter_malala?language=en

Thelma & Louise (1991) - IMDb. (n.d.). Retrieved from https://www.imdb.com/title/tt0103074.

Tippett, Constance. Goddess Timeline …because the feminine is simply divine. (n.d.). Retrieved from http://goddesstimeline.com/

Tolle, E. (2006). *A New Earth: Awakening to Your Life's Purpose*. Penguin.

Version, N. I. (2011). *NIV Bible eBook (New International Version)*. Hachette UK.

Yousafzai, M. (2013). *I am Malala: The Girl Who Stood up for Education and Was Shot by the Taliban*. Little, Brown.

Keep Your Quest On!

hank you for reading my book. It has been such a thrill and privilege to share with you! If you feel inspired to keep on questing and growing and inspiring, here are six great ideas:

1. **Join my Oranges for Eve Book Club**! I lead this book club in person and online.
   - Become exceedingly brave!
   - Deepen your connection to the Feminine Divine.
   - Create deep, nourishing connections with other people who share your spiritual path.
   - Do your "Spiritual Exercises" with my support and the encouragement of other loving people who share your journey.

   The book itself is a fantastic book club guide as it is full of powerful questions and specific exercises. Join the Oranges for Eve community and learn more www.facebook.com/groups/orangesforevebookclub.

2. **Create your own Oranges for Eve book club!** Use the exercises in this book as a guide for your meetings... and invite me! I would love to attend remotely or, if possible, in person.

3. **Take my Oranges for Eve online class:** This class is a go-at-your-own pace, warm, dive into feminine spirituality. Through powerful musical experiences, key

imagery and guided meditation, you will develop your own rich relationship with Eve and fully discover how the Feminine Divine lives in you. You will receive specific tools and practices to apply to your life right now!

There are gorgeous downloadable worksheets for your "Divine Home-work." This includes audio clips, which come with companion worksheets. During the course, we will have the opportunity to interact in a private Facebook group and LIVE through an online platform, which I will give you all the information about once you begin the course.

4. **Work with me one-on-one or in a small group.** I would be so honored to support you on your journey to grow your wings. As I am able, I open space for new clients. To connect with me about working together, please email me at rabbikolton@gmail.com

5. **Be a spiritual activist.** As Nancy Pelosi said, "We don't agonize, we organize!" Take your activism to the women's movement. March, donate, vote, volunteer and make your voice heard! Let your spiritual values lead your choices.

6. **Listen and feel.** In your own way, as you feel Her coming through to you, answer the call of the Feminine Divine. Your energy is needed on planet Earth right now. There are many, many solutions to ease the pain and suffering that we feel as individuals, as women and as a species. Do not be discouraged. Stay awake. Be brave. Fly.

Contact

Email: rabbikolton@gmail.com
Website: rabbikolton.com
Facebook: www.facebook.com/tamarakolton
Facebook: www.facebook.com/orangesforeve

**If you have enjoyed this book, I would deeply appreciate it
if you would take a moment and leave a review on Amazon.**

*~With Gratitude and Love
Rabbi Tamara Kolton*

About the Author

R abbi Tamara Kolton Ph.D. is an independent rabbi, psychologist, author and feminine mythologist. As a prominent rabbi in Michigan, she is known for her warm, inspirational style and deep capacity to help people heal.

For over 20 years, she has shared life's greatest joy and deepest sorrow with thousands of people. She officiates weddings locally and nationally, bringing warmth, dynamism and inclusivity to every ceremony. Closest to her heart, is her work with families as she tenderly and skillfully conducts funerals and offers comfort to those enduring loss.

Rabbi Kolton completed her undergraduate degree in Jerusalem from Hebrew University and she is a fluent Hebrew speaker. Her master's degree is in clinical psychology. She is a Ph.D. and wrote her dissertation on The Experience of Being a Woman Rabbi.

In 1999, Tamara was the first person to be ordained a humanistic rabbi, an achievement recognized by The New York Times. She is included in the historical timeline of women rabbis.

Tamara grew up in a Jewish congregation "without God" and was mentored by Rabbi Sherwin T. Wine, a radical and renowned rabbi. Ultimately, she became his successor and the senior rabbi at the very congregation where she grew up.

In 2012, she felt an intense spiritual yearning to discover God for herself and set out on a brave quest. In searching for "Him," she found "Her."

Today Rabbi Kolton is most passionate about the Feminine Divine and how to bring Her energy to a world in desperate need of feminine truth, light and power. She asks us to see Eve, of the bible, as a heroine and an unabashed powerhouse of beauty and bravery.

She asks us to see ourselves that way, too.

Rabbi Kolton is a member the International Women's Forum, a global leadership initiative that connects the world's most preeminent women of significant achievement.

She is the author of the new release, ***Oranges for Eve: My Brave, Beautiful, Badass Journey to the Feminine Divine.***

She is married to her Israeli-born husband and the mother of two teenagers. They live in Birmingham, Michigan with their Havanese dog, Finley.

Connect with her at rabbikolton.com

CPSIA information can be obtained
at www.ICGtesting.com
Printed in the USA
JSHW020735021219
2722JS00002B/3